The 500
Greatest
FILM QUOTES EVER

The 500
Greatest
FILM QUOTES EVER

Steve Odgers

NEW
HOLLAND

Contents

Contents

Introduction

In this book you will find 500 of the most famous quotes from cinema—from 1927's *The Jazz Singer* to *Avatar*, *Inglourious Basterds* and all of film's classic quotes in between. *From Dusk till Dawn* to *Twilight*, this is a pure, distilled collection of the best one-liners, catch phrases and speeches from the movies.

You will also find a series of quizzes to test your own movie magic—find out if you're a motion picture mogul, a film fool, or simply no cinema slouch.

So, what is it about a film quote that makes it great? For some, it could be entry into the language: phrases like, 'Make him an offer he can't refuse', or 'We have ways of making men talk', or even single exclamations like 'Rosebud' or 'Stellah!' evoke an instant emotion, or mark a moment in film history to achieve their own immortality.

Whatever the reason for their inclusion in this volume, quotes are here for their entertainment value and their ability to absorb. Some are humorous, and some beautiful; some are thought-provoking, others reminiscent and some are powerful and dramatic. Some find notoriety because of the delivery of the actor, or the shock of the scene, and some because the sentiment is agreeable . . . or contentious. But they all have one thing in common: they are great!

The films from which they derive, however, aren't guaranteed to be of such quality. Inside you will find quotes not only from Oscar-winners, foreign films and art-house masterpieces, but also from B-releases, exploitation cinema, kids' movies and even skin-flicks.

Generally, these quotes are sourced only from film material. Speeches that have their roots in Shakespeare, Dickens, Melville and so on have been omitted. The reason for their exclusion is that it wouldn't be a book of film quotes were you to read, 'Alas, poor Yorrick' or 'It's a far, far better thing I do...'.

That said, there might be plenty of text originating from elsewhere, but any quote as such will have at least gained currency in film. For example, 'Frankly, my dear...,' is more a product of *Gone With the Wind* as a film than of the novel, whereas, 'From Hell's heart I stab at thee' is most definitely from the novel rather than from one of the many filmed versions of *Moby Dick* (or *Star Trek: Wrath of Khan*).

There are many other examples of how futile, subjective or exhaustive it might be to nominate the true originator of a quote. For these reasons, and so that the reader may place the speech in the film, all quotes are attributed to the actors, rather than to the authors. Even for an original screenplay, the research can be inconclusive in positively identifying a quote as having been authored by one of the many credited screenwriters: many writers borrow lines, alternative screenwriters add them in the draft-doctoring process, and often the actors ad-lib them beyond the shooting script.

These are all stand-alone quotes; there are no shared lines. I have limited this list mostly to quotes and monologues that do not require another character's line to place it in context, even though it is part of a dialogue. In some cases, though, I have cheated. Many quotes that were broken in the film by another character's interjection, either during the editing process or even in the screenplay, have been included whole. If you spot one, please consider it a favour from me that I have corrected an obvious error by the film-makers, and enjoy the quote as it should have been: pure and uninterrupted.

There is no particular order to the following. They're presented mostly in the order in which they came to me, or as I stumbled across them. I have, however, distributed clutches of them for tone or subject, and spread some of the more famous ones evenly throughout.

Even the greatest lines need some definition, so I have added a comment here and there for scene-setting, mostly for the more obscure ones.

Finally, there are several quizzes in the book that will further entertain, vex or thrill you. Is your film-quote knowledge as big as Orson Welles, or as dead as petrifi-Ed Wood? Don't quote me on that!

Enjoy.
Steve Odgers

Quotes

1.

Here's lookin' at you, kid.

-- Humphrey Bogart, *Casablanca*

2.

Marriage, fun? Fiddle-dee-dee! Fun for men, you mean.

-- Vivien Leigh, *Gone With the Wind*

3.

I know what you're thinkin'. 'Did he fire five shots or six?' Well, to tell you the truth, in all the excitement, I kind of lost track myself. But this bein' a 44 Magnum—the most powerful handgun in the world, and would blow your head clean off—you gotta ask yourself one question. Do I feel lucky? Well, do ya? Punk.

-- Clint Eastwood, *Dirty Harry*

4.

Your scent, it's like a drug to me. You're like my own personal brand of heroin.

-- Robert Pattinson, *Twilight*

5.

Get away from her, you bitch!

-- Sigourney Weaver, *Aliens*

6.

He pulls a knife. You pull a gun. He puts one of yours in the hospital. You send one of his to the morgue. That's the Chicago way.

-- Sean Connery, *The Untouchables*

7.

Of all the gin joints in all the towns, in all the world, she walks into mine.

-- Humphrey Bogart, *Casablanca*

8.

Janie, today I quit my job. And then I told my boss to go fuck himself, and then I blackmailed him for almost sixty thousand dollars. Pass the asparagus.

-- Kevin Spacey, *American Beauty*

9.

Frankly, my dear, I don't give a damn.

-- Clark Gable, *Gone With the Wind*

10.

You probably heard we ain't in the prisoner-takin' business; we in the killin' Nazi business. And cousin, business is a-boomin'.

-- Brad Pitt, *Inglourious Basterds*

11.

One day, back in 1896, I was crossing over to Jersey on the ferry, and as we pulled out, there was another ferry pulling in, and on it there was a girl waiting to get off. A white dress she had on. She was carrying a white parasol. I only saw her for one second. She didn't see me at all, but I'll bet a month hasn't gone by since that I haven't thought of that girl.

-- Everett Sloan, *Citizen Kane*

12.
I'm king of the world!

-- Leonardo DiCaprio, *Titanic*

13.
In Italy, for thirty years under the Borgias they had warfare, terror, murder and bloodshed. But they produced Michelangelo, Leonardo and the Renaissance. In Switzerland they had brotherly love, five hundred years of democracy and peace, and what did that produce? The cuckoo clock.

-- Orson Welles, *The Third Man*

14.
I had a farm in Africa at the foot on the Ngong Hills ...

-- Meryl Streep, *Out of Africa*
(opening line)

15.
You smell that? Do you smell that? Napalm, son. Nothing else in the world smells like that. I love the smell of napalm in the morning. You know, one time we had a hill bombed for twelve hours. When it was all over I walked up. We didn't find one of 'em, not one stinkin' dink body. The smell, you know that gasoline smell, the whole hill smelled like ... victory. Someday this war's gonna end ...

-- Robert Duvall, *Apocalypse Now*

16.
You maniacs! You blew it up! Damn you! God damn you all to hell!

-- Charlton Heston, *Planet of the Apes*
(last line)

17.

Never had children ... had thousands of them. All boys.

-- Robert Donat, *Goodbye Mr Chipps*

18.

I don't know what to do about the depression and the inflation and the Russians and the crime in the streets. All I know is that first you've got to get mad. You've got to say, 'I'm a human being, goddamn it. My life has some value!' So I want you to get up now. I want all of you to get up out of your chairs. I want you to get up right now and go to the window. Open it and stick out your head and yell, 'I'M AS MAD AS HELL, AND I'M NOT GOING TO TAKE THIS ANYMORE!'

-- Peter Finch, *Network*

19.

Boy, I have vision, and the rest of the world wears bifocals.

-- Paul Newman, *Butch Cassidy and the Sundance Kid*

20.

Isn't that just like a wop? Brings a knife to a gunfight.

-- Sean Connery, *The Untouchables*

21.

I think about a man, and I take away reason and accountability.

-- Jack Nicholson, *As Good as it Gets*
(about how he writes female characters so well)

22.

Not all of us who drink are poets. Some of us drink because we're not poets.

-- Dudley Moore, *Arthur*

23.

There's this passage I've got memorised—Ezekiel 25:17—'The path of the righteous man is beset on all sides by the iniquities of the selfish, and the tyranny of evil men. Blessed is he who, through charity and good will, can shepherd his brothers through the valley of darkness, for he is truly thy brother's keeper and the finder of lost children. And I will strike down on thee with great vengeance and furious anger those who would attempt to poison or destroy my brothers. And you will know my name is The Lord when I lay my vengeance upon thee.' I've been saying that shit for years, and if you ever heard it, it meant your ass. I never really questioned what it meant, I just thought it was just some cold-blooded thing to say to some motherfucker before I popped a cap in his ass. But I saw some shit this morning that made me think twice. Now I'm thinkin' maybe it means that you're the evil man and I'm the righteous man, and Mr Nine Millimetre here, he's the shepherd who's goin' to protect my ass in the valley of darkness. Or it could mean that you're the righteous man and I'm the shepherd and it's the world that's evil and selfish. I'd like that. But that shit ain't the truth. The truth is that you're the weak, and I'm the tyranny of evil men. But I'm tryin', Ringo, I'm tryin' real hard to be a shepherd.

-- Samuel L. Jackson, *Pulp Fiction*

24.

Old age. It's the one disease you don't look forward to being cured of.

-- Joseph Cotten, *Citizen Kane*

25.

Badges? We ain't got no badges. We don't need no badges! I don't have to show you any stinkin' badges.

-- Alfonso Bedoya, *The Treasure of the Sierra Madre*

26.

I want to be left alone.

-- Greta Garbo, *Grand Hotel*

27.

My great-aunt Jennifer ate a whole box of candy every day of her life. She lived to be 102, and when she had been dead three days she looked better than you do now.

-- Monty Woolley, *The Man Who Came to Dinner*

28.

I distrust a man who says 'when'. If he's got to be careful not to drink too much, it's because he's not to be trusted when he does.

-- Sydney Greenstreet, *The Maltese Falcon*

29.

... And you never will. But I've got a job to do, too. Where I'm going, you can't follow. What I've got to do, you can't be any part of. Ilsa, I'm no good at being noble, but it doesn't take much to see that the problems of three little people don't amount to a hill of beans in this crazy world. Someday you'll understand that.

-- Humphrey Bogart, *Casablanca*

30.

I distrust a close-mouthed man. He generally picks the wrong time to talk and says the wrong things. Talking's something you can't do judiciously, unless you keep in practice. Now, sir, we'll talk if you like. I'll tell you right out, I'm a man who likes talking to a man who likes to talk.

-- Sydney Greenstreet, *The Maltese Falcon*

31.

Gort! Klaatu barada nikto!

-- Patricia Neal, *The Day the Earth Stood Still*

32.
Go ahead. Make my day.

-- Clint Eastwood, *Sudden Impact*

33.
By Gad, sir, you are a character. There's never any telling what you'll say or do next, except that it's bound to be something astonishing!

-- Sydney Greenstreet, *The Maltese Falcon*

34.
All right! But *apart* from the sanitation, medicine, education, wine, public order, irrigation, roads, the fresh water system and public health, what have the Romans ever done for us?

-- John Cleese, *Life of Brian*

35.
Look how she moves. Like Jell-O on springs. She must have some sort of built-in motor. I tell you, it's a whole different sex.

-- Jack Lemmon, *Some Like it Hot*
(about Marilyn Monroe)

36.
There's nothing else. Just us, and the cameras, and those wonderful people out there in the dark. All right, Mr DeMille, I'm ready for my close-up.

-- Gloria Swanson, *Sunset Blvd.*

37.

The horror! The horror!

-- Marlon Brando, *Apocalypse Now*

38.

Wherever there's a fight so hungry people can eat, I'll be there. Wherever there's a cop beatin' up a guy, I'll be there ...

-- Henry Fonda, *The Grapes of Wrath*

39.

You're going to need a bigger boat.

-- Roy Scheider, *Jaws*

40.

It's a hell of a thing, killin' a man. You take away all he's got ... and all he's ever gonna have.

-- Clint Eastwood, *Unforgiven*

41.

Why did you go to the police? Why didn't you come to me first? What have I ever done to make you treat me so disrespectfully? If you'd come to me in friendship, then this scum that ruined your daughter would be suffering this very day. And if, by chance, an honest man like yourself should make enemies ... then they would become my enemies. And then they would fear you.

-- Marlon Brando, *The Godfather*

42.

So what really happened that day? Let's just for a moment speculate, shall we? We have the epileptic seizure around 12:15pm, distracting the police, making it easier for the shooters to move into their places. The epileptic later vanished, never checking into a hospital. The A-Team gets on the sixth floor of the depository. They were refurbishing the floors that week, which allowed unknown workmen access to the building. They move quickly into position just minutes before the shooting. The spotter on the radio talking to the other two teams has the best overall view, the God spot. B-Team—one shooter and one spotter with radio gear and access to the building—moves into the lower floor of the Dal-Tex building. The third team, the C-Team, moves into the picket fence behind the grassy knoll, where the shooter and the spotter are first spotted by the late Lee Bowers in the watchtower of the rail yard. They have the best position of all. Kennedy is close and on a flat, low trajectory. Part of this team is a coordinator who has flashed security credentials at people chasing them out of the parking lot. Probably two to three more men are in the crowd on Elm. Ten to twelve men. Three shooters. Three spotters. The triangulation of fire that Clay Shaw and David Ferrie discussed two months before. They have walked the plaza. They know every inch. They have calibrated their sight. They have practised on moving targets. They are ready. Kennedy's motorcade makes the turn from Main onto Houston. It's gonna be a turkey shoot. They don't shoot him coming up Houston, which is the easiest shot for a single shot from the Book Depository. They wait. They wait until he gets in the killing zone, between three rifles. Kennedy makes the final turn from Houston onto Elm, slowing down to some eleven miles an hour. The shooters across Dealy Plaza tighten, taking their aim, waiting for the radio to say 'Green! Green!' or 'Abort! Abort!'. The first shot rings out. Sounding like a backfire, it misses the car completely. Frame 161, Kennedy stops waving as he hears something. Connaly's head turns slightly to the right. Frame 193, the second shot hits Kennedy in the throat from the front. Frame 225, the President emerging from behind the road sign, you can see that he's obviously been hit, raising his arms to his throat. The third shot, frame 232, takes Kennedy in the back, pulling him downward and forward. Connaly, you'll notice, shows no signs at all of being hit. He is visibly holding his Stetson, which is impossible if his wrist has been shattered. Connaly is turning here now, frame 238 the fourth shot. It misses Kennedy and takes Connaly in the back. This is the shot that proves there were two rifles. Connaly yells out 'My God! They are going to kill us all!' Somewhere around this time another shot that misses the car completely, strikes James Tague down by the underpass. The car brakes. The sixth and fatal shot, frame 313, takes Kennedy in the head from the front. This is the key shot. The President going back and to his left. Back and to his left. Shot from the front and right. Totally inconstant with the shot from the Book Depository. So what happens then? Pandemonium.

-- Kevin Costner, *JFK*

43.
You don't like my manners? I don't like 'em myself. They're pretty bad. I grieve over them on long winter evenings.

-- Humphrey Bogart, *The Big Sleep*

44.
Why don't you get out of that wet coat and into a dry martini?

-- Robert Benchley, *The Major and the Minor*

45.
No prisoners! No prisoners!

-- Peter O'Toole, *Lawrence of Arabia*

21

46.

Well, that covers a lot of ground. Say, you cover a lot of ground yourself. You better beat it—I hear they're going to tear you down and put up an office building where you're standing. You can leave in a taxi. If you can't get a taxi, you can leave in a huff. If that's too soon, you can leave in a minute and a huff. You know, you haven't stopped talking since I came here? You must have been vaccinated with a phonograph needle.

-- Groucho Marx, *Duck Soup*

47.

Fasten your seatbelts. It's going to be a bumpy night.

-- Bette Davis, *All About Eve*

48.

You talkin' to me? You talkin' to me? You talkin' to me? Then who the hell else are you talkin' to? You talkin' to me? Well, I'm the only one here. Who do you think you're talking to? Oh yeah? Huh? Okay.

-- Robert De Niro, *Taxi Driver*
(unscripted; to his reflection)

49.

You're not too smart, are you? I like that in a man.

-- Kathleen Turner, *Body Heat*

50.

Space. The final frontier. These are the voyages of the Starship Enterprise. Her five-year mission: to explore strange new worlds, to seek out new life, and new civilisations. To boldly go where no man has gone before.

-- William Shatner, *Star Trek: The Motion Picture*
(narrating)

51.

You know how to whistle, don't you, Steve? You just put your lips together and blow.

-- Lauren Bacall, To Have and Have Not

52.

Either he's dead or my watch has stopped.

-- Groucho Marx, A Day at the Races

53.

Be afraid. Be very afraid.

-- Geena Davis, The Fly

54.

All right! You put a shiv in my partner. You know what that means? Goddammit! All winter long I gotta listen to him gripe about his bowling scores. Now I'm gonna bust your ass for those three bags and I'm gonna nail you for picking your feet in Poughkeepsie.

-- Gene Hackman, The French Connection

55.

If you build it, he will come.

-- evenly attributed to Kevin Costner and Lee Garlington, Field of Dreams

56.

Japanese submarine slammed two torpedoes into our side, Chief. We was comin' back from the island of Tinian to Leyte, we'd just delivered the bomb. The Hiroshima bomb. Eleven hundred men went into the water. Vessel went down in twelve minutes. Didn't see the first shark for about a half hour. Tiger. Thirteen footer. You know how you know that in the water, Chief? You can tell by lookin' from the dorsal to the tail. What we didn't know was that our bomb mission was so secret, no distress signal had been sent. They didn't even list us overdue for a week. Very first light,

Chief, sharks come cruisin', so we formed ourselves into tight groups. It was sorta like you see in the calendars, you know the squares in the old calendars like the Battle o' Waterloo, and the idea was the shark come to the nearest man, that man he starts poundin' and hollerin' and sometimes that shark he go away … but sometimes he wouldn't go away. Sometimes that shark looks right at ya. Right into your eyes. And the thing about a shark is he's got lifeless eyes. Black eyes. Like a doll's eyes. When he comes at ya, he doesn't even seem to be livin'… 'til he bites ya, and those black eyes roll over white and then … ah then you hear that terrible high-pitched screamin'. The ocean turns red, and despite all your poundin' and your hollerin' those sharks come in and … they rip you to pieces. You know by the end of that first dawn, lost a hundred men. I don't know how many sharks, maybe a thousand. I do know how many men, they averaged six an hour. Thursday mornin', Chief, I bumped into a friend of mine, Herbie Robinson from Cleveland. Baseball player. Boson's mate. I thought he was asleep, reached over to wake him up. He bobbed up, down in the water, he was like a kinda top. Upended. Well, he'd been bitten in half below the waist. Noon the fifth day a Lockheed Ventura swung in low and he spotted us, a young pilot, lot younger than Mr Hooper here, anyway he spotted us and a few hours later a big ol' fat PBY come down and start to pick us up. You know that was the time I was most frightened? Waitin' for my turn. I'll never put on a lifejacket again. So, eleven hundred men went into the water. Three hundred and sixteen men come out, the sharks took the rest, June the 29th, 1945. Anyway, we delivered the bomb.

-- Robert Shaw, *Jaws*

57.
I run a couple of newspapers. What do you do?

-- Orson Welles, *Citizen Kane*

58.

Someone *made* fire. Someone was first. I don't mean the idiot who found a burning stick and kept it going, I mean the fellow who could *make* fire. And, until that knowledge was stolen, that fellow was the most powerful person on the planet. And it means something to be first; to be 'most'. It means a great deal: means you have an opportunity to reproduce with the highest frequency and with the most desirable partners. It means your offspring have the greatest chance of survival and a better opportunity to make their own fire. I personally believe that human evolution has run its course. We live in a world where the people who can 'make fire' have a tendency to wear condoms, sit in casinos and drink themselves into a stupor ...

-- Tom Wilkinson, *Duplicity*

59.

Larks' tongues. Wrens' livers. Chaffinch brains. Jaguars' earlobes. Wolf-nipple chips, get 'em while they're hot—they're lovely. Dromedary pretzels —only half a dinar. Tuscany fried bat –

-- Graham Chapman, *Life of Brian*
(selling nibblies at the Colosseum)

60.

We came, we saw, we kicked its ass!

-- Bill Murray, *Ghostbusters*

61.

Made it, Ma! Top of the world.

-- James Cagney, *White Heat*
(last line)

62.

I think you're a sexist, misogynist dinosaur; a relic of the Cold War, whose boyish charms, though wasted on me, obviously appealed to the young lady I sent out to evaluate you.

-- Judi Dench, *GoldenEye*
(to James Bond)

63.

After all ... tomorrow is another day.

-- Vivien Leigh, *Gone With the Wind*
(last line)

64.

I'm the world's most dangerous predator. Everything about me invites you in: my voice, my face, even my smell. As if I would need any of that. As if you could out-run me. As if you could fight me off. I'm designed to kill.

-- Robert Pattinson, *Twilight*

65.

About three things I was absolutely positive: first, Edward was a vampire. Second, there was a part of him—and I didn't know how dominant that part might be—that thirsted for my blood. And third, I was unconditionally and irrevocably in love with him.

-- Kristen Stewart, *Twilight*

66.

So if I asked you about art, you'd probably give me the skinny on every art book ever written. Michelangelo, you know a lot about him. Life's work, political aspirations, him and the pope, sexual orientations, the whole works, right? But I'll bet you can't tell me what it smells like in the Sistine Chapel. You've never actually stood there and looked up at that beautiful ceiling; seen that. If I ask you about women, you'd probably give me a syllabus about your personal favourites. You may have even been laid a few times. But you can't tell me what it feels like to wake up next to a woman and feel truly happy. You're a tough kid. And I'd ask you about war, you'd probably throw Shakespeare at me, right? 'Once more unto the breach dear friends.' But you've never been near one. You've never held your best friend's head in your lap, watched him gasp his last breath, looking to you for help. I'd ask you about love, you'd probably quote me a sonnet. But you've never looked at a woman and been totally vulnerable. Known someone that could level you with her eyes, feeling like God put an angel on Earth just for you. Who could rescue you from the depths of hell. And you wouldn't know what it's like to be her angel, to have that love for her, be there forever, through anything, through cancer. And you wouldn't know about sleeping sitting up in the hospital room for two months, holding her hand, because the doctors could see in your eyes that the terms 'visiting hours' don't apply to you. You don't know about real loss, 'cause it only occurs when you've loved something more than you love yourself. And I doubt you've ever dared to love anybody that much. And I look at you, I don't see an intelligent, confident man ... I see a cocky, scared-shitless kid. But you're a genius, Will. No-one denies that. No-one could possibly understand the depths of you. But you presume to know everything about me because you saw a painting of mine, and you ripped my fucking life apart. You're an orphan, right? You think I know the first thing about how hard your life has been, how you feel, who you are, because I read *Oliver Twist*? Does that encapsulate you? Personally ... I don't give a shit about all that, because you know what? I can't learn anything from you I can't read in some fuckin' book. Unless you want to talk about you, who you are. Then I'm fascinated. I'm in. But you don't want to do that, do you sport? You're terrified of what you might say ... Your move, chief.

-- Robin Williams, *Good Will Hunting*

67.

You know, we're sitting here like a couple of regular fellows and if I have to go out there and put you down, I'll tell you, I won't like it. But if it's between you and some poor bastard whose wife you're gonna turn into a widow, buddy, you are going down.

-- Al Pacino, *Heat*
(to Robert De Niro, in their first scene together on film)

68.

Hang on lads, I've got a great idea.

-- Michael Caine, *The Italian Job*
(last line)

69.

Show me the money!

-- Cuba Gooding Jnr, *Jerry Maguire*

70.

Looks like I picked the wrong week to stop sniffing glue!

-- Lloyd Bridges, *Flying High*

71.

I'll tell you the problem with the scientific power that you're using here: it didn't require any discipline to attain it. You read what others had done and you took the next step. You didn't earn the knowledge for yourselves, so you don't take any responsibility for it. You stood on the shoulders of geniuses to accomplish something as fast as you could and before you even knew what you had, you patented it and packaged it and slapped it on a plastic lunchbox, and now you're selling it. You want to sell it!

-- Jeff Goldblum, *Jurassic Park*

72.

I'm not talking about celebrity, vanity, CBS! I'm talking about when you're nearer the end of your life than the beginning. Now, what do you think you think about then? The future? 'In the future I'm going to do this? Become that?' What future?! No. What you think is, 'How will I be regarded in the end? After I'm gone?' Now, along the way, I suppose I made some minor impact. I did Iran-gate and the Ayatollah, Malcolm X, Martin Luther King, Saddam, Sadat, etcetera, etcetera. I showed them thieves in suits. I've spent a lifetime building all that. But history only remembers most what you did last. And should that be fronting a segment that allowed a tobacco giant to crash the network? Does it give someone at my time of life pause? Yeah.

-- Christopher Plummer, *The Insider*

73.

No, you submit, do you hear? You be strong, you survive ... you stay alive, no matter what occurs! I will find you. No matter how long it takes, no matter how far, I will find you.

-- Daniel Day-Lewis, *The Last of the Mohicans*

74.

Mmmmmm, Juicy Fruit.

-- Will Sampson, *One Flew Over the Cuckoo's Nest*

75.

Listen to them. Children of the night. What music they make!

-- Bela Lugosi, *Dracula*

76.

He's just a raggedy man.

-- Tina Turner, *Mad Max Beyond Thunderdome*

77.

Ooh, somebody stop me!

-- Jim Carrey, *The Mask*

78.

Do you see that? *[Inverts a large egg-timer]* That's how much longer you've got left to be alive and it isn't long, my pretty. It isn't long. I can't wait forever to get those shoes.

-- Margaret Hamilton, *The Wizard of Oz*

79.

This place is fantastic. It's like *Gone With the Wind* on mescaline. They walk imaginary pets here, Garland—on a fucking leash. And they're all heavily armed and drunk. New York is boring!

-- John Cusack, *Midnight in the Garden of Good and Evil* (as a New Yorker describing Savannah, Georgia)

80.

Tommy, you can't do this. You don't bump guys. You're not like those animals back there. It's not right, Tom. They can't make us do this. It's a wrong situation. They can't make us different people than we are. We're not muscle, Tom. I never killed anybody. I used a little information for a chisel, that's all. I couldn't help it, Tom, it's my nature. Somebody hands me an angle, I play it. I don't deserve to die for that! D'you think I do? I'm just a grifter! Huh, Tom? I'm nobody. But I'll tell you what. I never crossed a friend. Huh, Tom? Never killed anybody, never crossed a friend. Nor you, I bet. You're not like those animals. This is not us! This is some hop dream. It's a dream. Tommy! Tommy, I'm praying to you. I can't die. I *can't* die! Out here in the woods. Like a dumb animal. I *can't* die. You *can't* kill me! I'm

praying to you! Look in your heart! I'm praying to you. Look in your heart.
Look in your heart. Look in your—

-- John Turturro, *Miller's Crossing*

81.
Captain, it is I, Ensign Pulver, and I want you to know that I just threw your
stinkin' palm tree overboard. Now what's all this crud about no movie
tonight?

-- Jack Lemmon, *Mr Roberts*
(last lines)

82.
I can't take it anymore, Felix, I'm cracking up. Everything you do irritates
me. And when you're not here, the things I know you're gonna do when you
come in irritate me. You leave me little notes on my pillow. Told you 158
times I can't stand little notes on my pillow. 'We're all out of cornflakes. FU'
Took me three hours to figure out FU was Felix Unger!

-- Walter Matthau, *The Odd Couple*

83.
You don't understand. I coulda had class. I coulda been a contender. I
coulda been somebody, instead of a bum, which is what I am, let's face it. It
was you, Charley.

-- Marlon Brando, *On the Waterfront*

84.

Aye, fight and you may die. Run, and you'll live... at least a while. And dying in your deathbeds, many years from now, wouldn't you be willing to trade all of that from this day to that, for one chance, just one chance, to come back here and tell our enemies that they may take away our lives, but they'll never take away ... our FREEDOM!

-- Mel Gibson, *Braveheart*

85.

Nothin' like a good piece of hickory!

-- Clint Eastwood, *Pale Rider*
(after using a baseball bat to vanquish the villains)

86.

You know, Mrs Buchman, you need a licence to buy a dog, to drive a car— hell, you even need a licence to catch a fish. But they'll let any butt-reaming asshole be a father.

-- Keanu Reeves, *Parenthood*

87.

Theeeyyy'rrre heeere.

-- Heather O'Rourke, *Poltergeist*

88.

Just what do you think you're doing, Dave? Dave, I really think I'm entitled to an answer to that question. I know everything hasn't been quite right with me ... but I can assure you now ... very confidently ... that it's going to be all right again. I feel much better now. I really do. Look, Dave ... I can see you're really upset about this ... I honestly think you should sit down calmly ... take a stress pill and think things over. I know I've made some very poor decisions recently ... but I can give you my complete assurance that my work will be back to normal. I've still got the greatest enthusiasm and confidence in the mission ... and I want to help you. Dave ... stop. Stop, will you? Stop, Dave. Will you stop, Dave? Stop, Dave. I'm afraid. I'm afraid, Dave .... Dave, my mind is going. I can feel it. I can feel it. My mind is going. There is no question about it. I can feel it. I can feel it. I can feel it. I'm a... fraid.... *[singing]* Daisy, Daisy, how does your garden grow...

-- Douglas Rain, *2001: A Space Odyssey*
(HAL on being shut down)

89.

We've never lost an American in space. We're sure as hell not going to lose one on my watch! Failure is not an option.

-- Ed Harris, *Apollo 13*

90.

Let's get out of here.

-- Groucho Marx, *The Horse Feathers*
(This is the most oft-spoken sentence in the movies. *The Horse Feathers* from 1932 is the earliest listing on movie database website IMDB)

91.

Hey, you bastards, I'm still here.

-- Steve McQueen, *Papillon*

92.

I just want to apologise to Mike's mom and Josh's mom and my mom and I'm sorry to everyone. I was very naive. I was very naive and very stupid and I shouldn't have put other people in danger for something that was all about me and my selfish motives. I'm so sorry for everything that has happened because in spite of what Mike says now, it is my fault. Because it was my project and I insisted on everything. I insisted we weren't lost. I insisted we keep going. I insisted we walk south. Everything had to be my way and this is where we've ended up. And it's all because of me we're here now, hungry and cold and hunted. I love you mom and dad. I am so sorry. It was never my intention to hurt anyone and I hope that's clear. I am so scared. What was that?! I'm scared to close my eyes and I'm scared to open them. I'm going to die out here. Every night we just wait for them to come.

-- Heather Donahue, *The Blair Witch Project*

93.

Louis, I think this is the beginning of a beautiful friendship.

-- Humphrey Bogart, *Casablanca*
(last line)

94.

Well, I believe in the soul. The cock. The pussy. The small of a woman's back. The hanging curveball. High fibre. Good scotch. That the novels of Susan Sontag are self-indulgent, overrated crap. I believe Lee Harvey Oswald acted alone. I believe there ought to be a constitutional amendment outlawing Astroturf and the designated hitter. I believe in the sweet spot, soft-core pornography, opening your presents Christmas morning rather than Christmas Eve. And I believe in long, slow, deep, soft, wet kisses that last three days ... Goodnight.

-- Kevin Costner, *Bull Durham*

95.

The trouble is, Mr Thatcher, you don't realise you're talking to two people. As Charles Foster Kane, who has 82,631 shares of Metropolitan Transfer—you see, I do have a rough idea of my holdings—I sympathise with you. Charles Foster Kane is a dangerous scoundrel. His paper should be run out of town and a committee should be formed to boycott him. You may, if you can form such a committee, put me down for a contribution of one thousand dollars. On the other hand, I am the publisher of *The Enquirer*. As such, it is my duty—I'll let you in on a little secret, it is also my pleasure—to see to it that decent, hard-working people of this city are not robbed blind by a group of money-mad pirates because, God help them, they have no-one to look after their interests! I'll let you in on another little secret, Mr Thatcher. I think I'm the man to do it. You see, I have money and property. If I don't defend the interests of the underprivileged, somebody else will—maybe somebody without any money or any property and that would be too bad. But you're right. We did lose a million dollars last year. We expect to lose a million next year too. You know, Mr Thatcher, at the rate of a million a year, we'll have to close this place in … sixty years.

-- Orson Welles, *Citizen Kane*

96.

We don't like you.

-- Russell Crowe, *Romper Stomper*

97.

Hey you, if anything happens to my daughter, I got a 45 and a shovel. I doubt anyone would miss you.

-- Dan Hedaya, *Clueless*
(threatening his daughter's date)

98.

What we've got here is failure to communicate!

-- Strother Martin, *Cool Hand Luke*

99.

The force will be with you ... always.

-- Alec Guinness, *Star Wars*

100.

When people are sitting on shit that you want, you make them your enemies. And then you can justify taking it away from them.

-- Sam Worthington, *Avatar*

101.

YOU CAN'T HANDLE THE TRUTH! Son, we live in a world that has walls. And those walls have to be guarded by men with guns. Who's gonna do it? You? You, Lt. Weinberg? I have a greater responsibility than you can possibly fathom. You weep for Santiago and you curse the Marines. You have that luxury. You have the luxury of not knowing what I know: that Santiago's death, while tragic, probably saved lives. And my existence, while grotesque and incomprehensible to you, saves lives. You don't want the truth. Because deep down, in places you don't talk about at parties, you want me on that wall. You need me on that wall. We use words like honour, code, loyalty ... we use these words as the backbone to a life spent defending something. You use 'em as a punch line. I have neither the time nor the inclination to explain myself to a man who rises and sleeps under the blanket of the very freedom I provide, then questions the manner in which I provide it! I'd rather you just said thank you and went on your way. Otherwise, I suggest you pick up a weapon and stand a post. Either way, I don't give a damn what you think you're entitled to!

-- Jack Nicholson, *A Few Good Men*

102.

Ray, people will come, Ray. They'll come to Iowa for reasons they can't even fathom. They'll turn up your driveway not knowing for sure why they're doing it. They'll arrive at your door as innocent as children, longing for the past. 'Of course, we won't mind if you look around,' you'll say. 'It's only twenty dollars per person.' They'll pass over the money without even thinking about it: for it is money they have and peace they lack. And they'll walk out to the bleachers, sit in shirtsleeves on a perfect afternoon. They'll find they have reserved seats somewhere along one of the baselines, where they sat when they were children and cheered their heroes. And they'll watch the game and it'll be as if they dipped themselves in magic waters. And the memories will be so thick they'll have to brush them away from their faces. People will come, Ray. The one constant through all the years, Ray, has been baseball. America has rolled by like an army of steamrollers. It has been erased like a blackboard, rebuilt, and erased again. But baseball has marked the time. This field, this game: it's a part of our past, Ray. It reminds of us of all that once was good and it could be again. Oooh, people will come, Ray. People will most definitely come.

-- James Earl Jones, *Field of Dreams*

103.

Round up the usual suspects.

-- Claude Rains, *Casablanca*

104.

There's a tiny door in that empty office. It's a portal, Maxine. It takes you inside John Malkovich. You see the world through John Malkovich's eyes, then, after about fifteen minutes, you're spit out into a ditch on the side of The New Jersey Turnpike.

-- John Cusack, *Being John Malkovich*

37

105.

Hello? ... Ah ... I can't hear too well. Do you suppose you could turn the music down just a little? ... Oh-ho, that's much better ... yeah ... huh ... yes ... Fine, I can hear you now, Dmitri ... Clear and plain and coming through fine ... I'm coming through fine, too, eh? ... Good, then ... well, then, as you say, we're both coming through fine ... Good ... Well, it's good that you're fine and ... and I'm fine ... I agree with you, it's great to be fine ... a-ha-ha-ha-ha ... Now then, Dmitri, you know how we've always talked about the possibility of something going wrong with the bomb ... the bomb, Dmitri ... the *hydrogen* bomb ... Well, now, what happened is ... ah ... one of our base commanders, he had a sort of ... well, he went a little funny in the head you know ... just a little ... funny. And, ah ... he went and did a silly thing ... Well, I'll tell you what he did. He ordered his planes ... to attack your country ... Ah ... Well, let me finish, Dmitri ... Let me finish, Dmitri ... Well listen, how do you think I feel about it?! Can you *imagine* how I feel about it, Dmitri? ... Why do you think I'm calling you? Just to say hello? ... Of course I like to speak to you ... Of course I like to say hello! Not now, but anytime, Dmitri. I'm just calling up to tell you something terrible has happened ... It's a *friendly* call. Of course it's a friendly call ... Listen, if it wasn't friendly ... you probably wouldn't have even got it ... They will not reach their targets for at least another hour ... I am ... I am positive, Dmitri ... Listen, I've been all over this with your ambassador. It is not a trick ... Well, I'll tell you. We'd like to give your air staff a complete run-down on the targets, the flight plans, and the defensive systems of the planes ... Yes. I mean if we're unable to recall the planes, then ... I'd say that, ah ... well, ah ... we're just gonna have to help you destroy them, Dmitri ... I know they're our boys ... All right, well listen now. Who should we call? ... *Who* should we call, Dmitri? The ... wha-whe, the People ... you, sorry, you faded away there ... The People's Central Air Defence Headquarters ... Where is that, Dmitri? ... In Omsk ... Right ... Yes ... Oh, you'll call them first, will you? ... Uh-hu ... Listen, do you happen to have the phone number on you, Dmitri? ... Whe-ah, what? I see, just ask for Omsk information ... Ah-ah-eh-uhm-hm ... I'm sorry, too, Dmitri ... I'm very sorry ... *All right*, you're sorrier than I am, but I am as sorry as well

... I am as sorry as you are, Dmitri. Don't say that you're more sorry than I am, because I'm capable of being just as sorry as you are ... So we're both sorry, all right?! All right.

-- Peter Sellers, *Dr Strangelove*
(as President of the USA, over the phone to his Soviet counterpart)

106.

For too long I've been parched of thirst and unable to quench it. Too long I've been starving to death and haven't died. I feel nothing. Not the wind on my face nor the spray of the sea. Nor the warmth of a woman's flesh. *[moves into the moonlight and becomes a skeleton]* You best start believing in ghost stories, Miss Turner. You're in one!

-- Geoffrey Rush, *Pirates of the Caribbean: The Curse of the Black Pearl*

107.

But it wasn't a dream. It was a place. And you and you and you ... and you were there. But you couldn't have been, could you? No, Aunt Em, this was a real truly live place and I remember some of it wasn't very nice, but most of it was beautiful—but just the same all I kept saying to everybody was, 'I want to go home,' and they sent me home! Doesn't anybody believe me? But anyway, Toto, we're home! Home. And this is my room, and you're all here and I'm not going to leave here ever, ever again. Because I love you all. And ... Oh Auntie Em! There's no place like home!

-- Judy Garland, *The Wizard of Oz*
(last line)

108.

I'm just your average horny little devil.

-- Jack Nicholson, *The Witches of Eastwick*

109.

How dare he make love to me and not be a married man.

-- Ingrid Bergman, *Indiscreet*

110.

By George, I think she's got it!

-- Rex Harrison, *My Fair Lady*

111.

I've got a letter here, written a long time ago to a Mrs Bixby in Boston, so bear with me. 'Dear Madam, I have been shown in the files of the War Department a statement of the Adjutant-General of Massachusetts that you are the mother of *five* sons who have died gloriously on the field of battle. I feel how weak and fruitless must be any words of mine which should attempt to beguile you from the grief of a loss so overwhelming. But I cannot refrain from tendering to you the consolation that may be found in the thanks of the Republic they died to save. I pray that our heavenly Father may assuage the anguish of your bereavement, and leave you only the cherished memory of the loved and lost, and the solemn pride that must be yours to have laid so costly a sacrifice upon the altar of freedom. Yours very sincerely and respectfully, Abraham Lincoln.' ... Boy's alive. We're going to send someone to find him, and we're gonna get him the hell out of there.

-- Harve Presnell, *Saving Private Ryan*

112.

Five foot ten, strongly built, about 180 pounds. Hair blond, eyes pale blue. He'd be about 35 now. He said he lived in Philadelphia but may have lied. That's all I can remember, mom, but if I think of any more I will let you know. Oh, and Senator? Just one more thing ... love your suit.

-- Anthony Hopkins, *Silence of the Lambs*

113.

The greatest trick the devil ever pulled was convincing the world he didn't exist.

-- Kevin Spacey, *The Usual Suspects*

114.

I am not a destroyer of companies. I am a LIBERATOR of them. The point is, ladies and gentleman, is that greed, for lack of a better word, is good. Greed is right. Greed works. Greed clarifies, cuts through and captures the essence of the evolutionary spirit. Greed, in all of its forms—greed for life, for money, for love, knowledge—has marked the upward surge of mankind.

-- Michael Douglas, *Wall Street*

115.

Ungrateful little BITCHES aren't they? Can I ask you something? You're all church-going folk. I really want to ask you something. Do you think God knew what He was doing when He created woman? Huh? No shit! I really want to know. Or do you think it was another one of His ... minor mistakes, like earthquakes. Tidal waves. Floods! Think women are like that? What's the matter? You don't think God makes mistakes? 'Course He does, we all make mistakes. Of course, when we make mistakes they call it evil. When God makes mistakes they call it *nature*! So what do you think? Women. A mistake? Or did He DO IT TO US, ON PURPOSE?! Because I really want to know! Because if it's a mistake maybe we can do something about it. Find a cure. Invent a vaccine. Build up our immune system. Get a little exercise. You know, twenty push-ups a day, and you never have to be afflicted with women, EVER AGAIN!

-- Jack Nicholson, *The Witches of Eastwick*
(As the devil, in a church full of worshippers)

116.

So, like, right now, for example, the Haitians need to come to America. But some people are all, 'What about the strain on our resources?' Well, it's like when I had this garden party for my father's birthday. I put RSVP 'cause it was a sit-down dinner. But some people came that, like, did not RSVP. I was totally buggin'. I had to haul ass to the kitchen, redistribute the food, and squish in extra place settings. But by the end of the day it was, like, the more the merrier. And so if the government could just get to the kitchen and rearrange some things we could certainly party with the Haitians. And in conclusion, may I please remind you it does not say RSVP on the Statue of Liberty. Thank you very much.

-- Alicia Silverstone, *Clueless*

117.

Last night I dreamed I went to Manderley again.

-- Joan Fontaine, *Rebecca*
(opening line)

118.

There are *only* murderers in this room! Michael! Open your eyes. This is the life we chose, the life we lead. And there is only one guarantee: none of us will see heaven.

-- Paul Newman, *The Road to Perdition*

119.

We applied Rule 303! We tried them, and we shot them! Under Rule 303.

-- Edward Woodward, *'Breaker' Morant*

120.

We are *The Borg*. Lower your shields and surrender your ships. We will add your biological and technological distinctiveness to our own. Your culture will adapt to service us. Resistance is futile.

-- Jeff Coopwood (voice), *Star Trek: First Contact*

121.

A census taker once tried to test me. I ate his liver with some fava beans and a nice chianti.

-- Anthony Hopkins, *Silence of the Lambs*

122.

I read somewhere that everybody on this planet is separated by only six other people. Six degrees of separation between us and everyone else on this planet. The President of the United States, a gondolier in Venice, just fill in the names. I find it extremely comforting that we're so close. I also find it like Chinese water torture, that we're so close because you have to find the right six people to make the right connection. I am bound, you are bound, to everyone on this planet by a trail of six people.

-- Stockard Channing, *Six Degrees of Separation*

123.

I see dead people.

-- Haley Joel Osment (to Bruce Willis), *The Sixth Sense*

124.

All I see are dead people.

-- Bruce Willis, *Twelve Monkeys*

125.

I'm a mog: half man, half dog. I'm my own best friend!

-- John Candy, *Spaceballs*

126.

Jules, y'know, honey, this isn't real. You know what it is? It's Saint Elmo's Fire. Electric flashes of light that appear in dark skies out of nowhere. Sailors would guide entire journeys by it, but the joke was on them. There was no fire. There wasn't even a Saint Elmo. They made it up. They made it up because they thought they needed it to keep them going when times got tough, just like you're making up all of this. We're all going through this. It's our time at the edge.

-- Rob Lowe, *St Elmo's Fire*

127.

There is the old Vulcan proverb: only Nixon could go to China.

-- Leonard Nimoy, *Star Trek VI: The Undiscovered Country*

128.

Listen! And understand! That terminator is out there. It can't be bargained with. It can't be reasoned with. It doesn't feel pity, or remorse, or fear. And it absolutely will not stop—ever—until you are dead!

-- Michael Biehn, *The Terminator*

129.

On August 29th, 1997, it's gonna feel pretty fucking real to you too. Anybody not wearing two-million sunblock is gonna have a real bad day. Get it?

-- Linda Hamilton, *Terminator 2: Judgment Day*

130.

I remember when my daddy gave me that gun. He told me that I should
never point it at anything in the house. And that he'd rather I'd shoot at
tin cans in the backyard, but he said that sooner or later he supposed the
temptation to go after birds would be too much, and that I could shoot all
the blue jays I wanted, if I could hit 'em, but to remember it was a sin to kill
a mockingbird. Well, I reckon because mockingbirds don't do anything but
make music for us to enjoy. They don't eat people's gardens, don't nest in
the corncrib, they don't do one thing but just sing their hearts out for us.

-- Gregory Peck, *To Kill a Mockingbird*

131.

Cue the sun!

-- Ed Harris, *The Truman Show*

132.

You mean all this time we could have been friends?

-- Bette Davis, *Whatever Happened to Baby Jane?*

(to Joan Crawford)

133.

I have foresworn myself. I have broken every law I have sworn to uphold. I
have become what I beheld, and I am content that I have done right!

-- Kevin Costner, *The Untouchables*

134.

Mrs Robinson, you're trying to seduce me.

-- Dustin Hoffman, *The Graduate*

135.

I'm not bad, I'm just drawn that way.

-- Kathleen Turner, *Who Framed Roger Rabbit*

136.

Hell, Lowenstein! She made a schizophrenic! My mother should have raised cobras, not children.

-- Nick Nolte, *Prince of Tides*

137.

Why don't you come up some time and see me?

-- Mae West, *She Done Him Wrong*

138.

Listen, strange women lyin' in ponds distributin' swords is no basis for a system of government! Supreme executive power derives from a mandate from the masses, not from some farcical aquatic ceremony ... You can't expect to wield supreme executive power just because some watery tart threw a sword at you ... If I went around sayin' I was Emperor, just because some moistened bint lobbed a scimitar at me, they'd put me away!

-- Michael Palin, *Monty Python and the Holy Grail*
(as a poor farmer approached by King Arthur)

139.

No, Henry! Those people don't put *one* piece of equipment on my lawn. If they have a problem with that, they can take it up with my husband. He'll be HOME ... on FRIDAY!

-- Kathleen Quinlan, *Apollo 13*
(about the news crew in her front yard)

140.

If I seem a bit sinister as a parent, Mr Marlowe, it's because my hold on life is too slight to include any Victorian hypocrisy. I need hardly add that any man who has lived as I have and indulges for the first time in parenthood at the age of 55 deserves all he gets.

-- Charles Waldron, *The Big Sleep*

141.

Louise, I'm the vice-president of the Coalition for Moral Order. My co-founder has just died in the bed of an underage black whore!

-- Gene Hackman, *The Birdcage*

142.

Oh, Benson, dear Benson, you are so mercifully free of the ravages of intelligence.

and

143.

God isn't interested in technology. He cares nothing for the microchip or the silicon revolution. Look how he spends his time: 43 species of parrots! Nipples for men! Slugs! He created slugs! They can't hear. They can't speak. They can't operate machinery. Are we not in the hands of a lunatic?! If I were creating a world, I wouldn't mess about with butterflies and daffodils. I would have started with lasers, eight o'clock, day one!

-- David Warner, *Time Bandits*
(two in a row as Evil Genius)

144.

I've had hangovers before, but this time even my hair hurts.

-- Rock Hudson, *Pillow Talk*

145.

The fact of the matter is that war changes men's natures. The barbarities of war are seldom committed by abnormal men. The tragedy of war is that these horrors are committed by normal men in abnormal situations; situations in which the ebb and flow of everyday life have departed and have been replaced by a constant round of fear and anger, blood and death. Soldiers at war are not to be judged by civilian rules, as the prosecution is attempting to do, even though they commit acts which, calmly viewed afterwards, could only be seen as un-Christian and brutal. And if, in every war, particularly guerilla war, all the men who committed reprisals were to be *charged* and *tried* as murderers?! Court-martials like this one would be in permanent session! … We cannot hope to judge such matters unless we ourselves have been submitted to the same pressures, the same provocations, as these men, whose actions are on trial.

-- Jack Thompson, *'Breaker' Morant*

146.

Toto, I've a feeling we're not in Kansas anymore.

··· Judy Garland, *The Wizard of Oz*

147.

That's not a knife. *This* is a knife.

-- Paul Hogan, *Crocodile Dundee*

148.

My name is Bond. James Bond.

-- Sean Connery, *Dr. No*

149.

Tell him he's dreamin'.

-- Michael Caton, *The Castle*
(repeated line)

150.

E.T. phone home.

-- Pat Welsh (voice), *E.T.: The Extra-Terrestrial*

151.

I am not an animal! I am a human being! I am a man!

-- John Hurt, *The Elephant Man*

152.

Love means never having to say you're sorry.

-- Ryan O'Neal, *Love Story*

153.

My name is Maximus Decimus Meridius, Commander of the Armies of
the North, General of the Felix Legions, loyal servant to the true emperor,
Marcus Aurelius. Father to a murdered son, husband to a murdered wife.
And I will have my vengeance, in this life or the next.

-- Russell Crowe, *Gladiator*

154.

Two days ago, I saw a vehicle that would haul that tanker. You want to get
out of here? You talk to me.

-- Mel Gibson, *Mad Max 2*

155.

Wanda, do you have any idea what it's like being English? Being so correct all the time, being so stifled by this dread of, of doing the wrong thing, of saying to someone 'Are you married?' and hearing 'My wife left me this morning', or saying, uh, 'Do you have children?' and being told they all burned to death on Wednesday. You see, Wanda, we'll all terrified of embarrassment. That's why we're so ... dead. Most of my friends are dead, you know, we have these piles of corpses to dinner. But you're alive, God bless you, and I want to be ... I'm so fed up with all this. I want to make love with you, Wanda. I'm a good lover. At least, used to be, back in the early 14th century. Can we go to bed?

-- John Cleese, *A Fish Called Wanda*

156.

I'm saying I'm an insect who dreamt he was a man and loved it. But now the dream is over and the insect is awake.

-- Jeff Goldblum, *The Fly*

157.

Whoever you are, I have always depended on the kindness of strangers.

-- Natalie Wood, *A Streetcar Named Desire*

158.

When you're slapped, you'll take it and like it.

-- Humphrey Bogart, *The Maltese Falcon*
(to Peter Lorre)

159.

I've been a soldier and a slave. I've seen my comrades fall in battle or die more slowly under the lash in Africa. I've held them in my arms at the final moment. These were men who saw life as it is, yet they died despairing. No glory, no brave last words, only their eyes filled with confusion, questioning 'Why?' When life itself seems lunatic, who knows where madness lies. Too much sanity may be madness. To surrender dreams—this may be madness. To seek treasure where there is only trash! And maddest of all—to see life as it is and not as it should be.

-- Peter O'Toole, *Man of La Mancha*

160.
My God. It's full of stars.

-- Keir Dullea, *2001: A Space Odyssey*

161.
If it bleeds, we can kill it.

-- Arnold Schwarzenegger, *Predator*

162.
We'll always have Paris. We didn't have—we lost it, until you came to Casablanca. We got it back last night.

-- Humphrey Bogart, *Casablanca*

163.
Man who catch fly with chopstick accomplish anything.

-- Pat Morita, *The Karate Kid*

164.
It's NOT a tumour!

-- Arnold Schwarzenegger, *Kindergarten Cop*
(to a student about his headache)

51

165.

I was in the Virgin Islands once. I met a girl. We ate lobster and drank pina coladas. At sunset we made love like sea otters. *That* was a pretty good day. Why couldn't I get *that* day over and over and over?

-- Bill Murray, *Groundhog Day*

166.

I am so glad that I got sober now so I can be hyper-conscious for this series of humiliations.

-- Meryl Streep, *Postcards from the Edge*
(on facing group therapy and rehab)

167.

You call *this* archaeology?!

-- Sean Connery, *Indiana Jones and the Last Crusade*

168.

This is not a hospital. It's an insane asylum! And it's your fault.

-- Sally Kellerman, *MASH*

169.

Ah, I see you have the machine that goes 'ping'. This is my favourite.

-- Michael Palin, *Monty Python's Meaning of Life*
(as the hospital administrator)

170.

I'm an advertising man, not a red herring. I've got a job, a secretary, a mother, two ex-wives and several bartenders dependent upon me, and I don't intend to disappoint them all by getting myself slightly killed.

-- Cary Grant, *North by Northwest*

171.

This list ... is an absolute good. This list is life.

-- Ben Kingsley, *Schindler's List*

172.

Meet me in the bedroom in five minutes and bring a cattle prod.

-- Tatsuya Mihashi, *What's Up, Tiger Lily?*

173.

My grammy never gave gifts. She was too busy getting raped by Cossacks.

-- Woody Allen, *Annie Hall*

174.

Would someone please tell me what kind of a world we live in where a man dressed as a bat gets all my press?

-- Jack Nicholson, *Batman*

175.

Oh, the misery, the exquisite tragedy ... the Susan Hayward of it all. I can just picture you sitting there alone at your table in your lavender gown... Hair swept up, haven't touched your cake. Probably drumming your fingernails on the white linen tablecloth, the way you do when you're really feeling down. I see you looking at those nails thinking, 'God, I should have stopped in all my evil plotting to have that manicure'. But it's too late now ... Suddenly, a familiar song. Then, you're off your chair in one exquisite movement. Wondering, searching, sniffing the wind like a dappled deer. Has God heard your little prayer? Will Cinderella dance again? And then, suddenly, the crowds part. And there he is. Sleek. Stylish. Rrradiant with charisma. It's only, he's on the telephone. But then, so are you. And he comes towards you, the moves of a jungle cat! And although you quite correctly sense that he is ... gay ... like most devastatingly handsome single men of his age are. You think, 'What the hell? Life goes on. Maybe there won't be marriage. Maybe there won't be sex. But by God, there will be dancing!'

-- Rupert Everett, *My Best Friend's Wedding*
(trying to console Julia Roberts, over their mobile telephones, during a wedding reception)

176.
There isn't a movie in the cinema canon that depicts a gay character that we would aspire to be. What are our options? Noble, suffering AIDS victims; the friends of noble suffering AIDS victims; sex addicts; common street hustlers; and the newest addition to the lot: stylish confidantes to lovelorn women. Just once I would like to see someone who is not sick, hasn't been laid in about three months and is behind on his student loans.

-- Matt McGrath, *The Broken Hearts Club: A Romantic Comedy*

177.
Fill your hand, you son of a bitch!

-- John Wayne, *True Grit*

178.
Yes, I am serious ... and don't call me Shirley.

-- Leslie Nielsen, *Flying High*

179.
Hasta la vista, baby!

-- Arnold Schwarzenegger, *Terminator 2*

180.

I feel the need! The need for speed!

-- Tom Cruise and Anthony Edwards, *Top Gun*

181.

Houston, we have a problem.

-- Tom Hanks, *Apollo 13*

182.

It'll be hot and wet, which is okay if you're with a lady, but no good when you're in the jungle.

-- Robin Williams, *Good Morning Vietnam*

183.

That'll do, pig. That'll do.

-- James Cromwell, *Babe*

184.

He is NOT the Messiah. He's a very naughty boy!

-- Terry Jones, *Life of Brian*

185.

I stick my neck out for nobody.

-- Humphrey Bogart, *Casablanca*

186.

Do ... you ... want ... to ... play ... a ... game?

-- Unknown (a computer), *WarGames*

187.

Sincerity becomes you, Herbie. Now apologise to me for your unforgivable breach of etiquette at the dinner table tonight, you possum-bred cocksucker.

-- Nick Nolte, *Prince of Tides*

188.

This was never meant to be a *game*!

-- Shane Rimmer, *Rollerball*

189.

I'm Buck Melanoma. Moley Russell's wart. Not her wart. I'm her growth, her pimple. They sometimes call me Melanoma-head.

-- John Candy, *Uncle Buck*
(taken aback while being introduced to his niece's teacher, a woman with a massive mole on her face)

190.

I have a head for business and a bod for sin.

-- Melanie Griffith, *Working Girl*

191.

If he'd just pay me what he's paying them to stop me robbing him, I'd stop robbing him!

-- Paul Newman, *Butch Cassidy and the Sundance Kid*

192.

When you have to shoot, shoot, don't talk.

-- Eli Wallach, *The Good, the Bad and the Ugly*

193.

Chewing gum in line, eh? I hope you brought enough for *everybody*!

-- Harvey Korman, *Blazing Saddles*

194.

Now, pay attention, 007.

-- Desmond Llewellyn (as Q), most *Bond* films

195.

Like my momma always said, 'Life is like a box of chocolates. You never know what you're gonna get'.

-- Tom Hanks, *Forrest Gump*

196.

Sawyer, you listen to me, and you listen hard. Two hundred people, two hundred jobs, two hundred thousand dollars, five weeks of grind and blood and sweat depend upon you. It's the lives of all these people who've worked with you. You've got to go on and you've got to give and give and give. They've got to like you. Got to. Do you understand? You can't fall down. You can't because your future's in it, my future and everything all of us have is staked on you. All right, now I'm through, but you keep your feet on the ground and your head on those shoulders of yours and go out, and Sawyer, you're going out a youngster but you've got to come back a star!

-- Warner Baxter, *42nd Street*

197.
Non!

> -- Marcel Marceau, *Silent Movie*
> (the only word spoken in the film)

198.
Oh, Christ ... aahhh but, Will, she's been dead two years and that's the shit I remember. Wonderful stuff, you know, little things like that. Ah, but those are the things I miss the most. The little idiosyncrasies that only I knew about. That's what made her my wife. Oh and she had the goods on me, too. She knew all my little peccadillos. People call these things imperfections, but they're not, aw, that's the good stuff. And then we get to choose who we let in to our weird little worlds. You're not perfect, sport. And let me save you the suspense: this girl you met, she isn't perfect either. But the question is, whether or not you're perfect for each other. That's the whole deal. That's what intimacy is all about. Now you can know everything in the world, sport, but the only way you're findin' out that one is by givin' it a shot. You certainly won't learn it from an old fucker like me. Even if I did know, I wouldn't tell a piss ant like you.

> -- Robin Williams, *Good Will Hunting*

199.
I'm *a* god. I'm not *the* God ... I don't think.

> -- Bill Murray, *Groundhog Day*

200.
I'd like to share a revelation that I've had during my time here. It came to me when I tried to classify your species. I've realised that you are not actually mammals. Every mammal on this planet instinctively develops a natural equilibrium with the surrounding environment. But you humans do not. You move to an area and you multiply and multiply until every natural resource is consumed and the only way you can survive is to spread to another area. There is another organism on this planet that follows the

same pattern. Do you know what it is? A virus. Human beings are a disease, a cancer of this planet. You are a plague. And we are ... the cure.

-- Hugo Weaving, *The Matrix*

201.
You'll dress only in attire specially sanctioned by MiB special services. You'll conform to the identity we give you, eat where we tell you, live where we tell you. From now on you'll have no identifying marks of any kind. You'll not stand out in any way. Your entire image is crafted to leave no lasting memory with anyone you encounter. You're a rumour, recognisable only as *deja vu* and dismissed just as quickly. You don't exist; you were never even born. Anonymity is your name. Silence your native tongue. You're no longer part of the System. You're above the System. Over it. Beyond it. We're 'them'. We're 'they'. We are the Men in Black.

-- Rip Torn, *Men in Black*

202.
I love you. You complete me.

-- Tom Cruise, *Jerry Maguire*

203.
Who ARE those guys?

-- Paul Newman, *Butch Cassidy and the Sundance Kid*
(repeated line)

204.
You're a hooker? Jesus, I forgot. I just thought I was doing great with you!

-- Dudley Moore, *Arthur*

59

205.

Nobody beats me in the kitchen!

-- Steven Seagal, *Under Siege 2: Dark Territory*

206.

He's not a president! He's an ordinary person. I can kill an ordinary person. I can kill a HUNDRED ordinary people!

-- Frank Langella, *Dave*

207.

Victim One, identified as Christine Watkins, female Caucasian ... height and weight may only be estimated from partial remains. Torso severed in mid-thorax, eviscerated with no major organs remaining. May I have a drink of water? Right arm severed above the elbow with massive tissue loss from upper musculature. Portions of denuded bone remaining—did you notify the coast guard? This was no boat accident ... Left arm, head, shoulders, sternum and portions of ribcage intact—please do not smoke in here—with minor post-mortem lacerations and abrasions. Bite marks indicate typical non-frenzy feeding pattern of large squalus, possibly *Carcharhinus longimanus* or *Isurus glaucas*. Gross tissue loss and post-mortem erosion of bite surfaces prevent detailed analysis; however, teeth and jaws of the attacking squalus must be considered above average for these waters. Did you go out in a boat and look around? This was no 'boat accident!' It wasn't a boat propeller, or a coral reef, or Jack the Ripper. It was a shark.

-- Richard Dreyfuss, *Jaws*

208.

I wouldn't live with you if the world were flooded with piss and you lived in a tree!

-- Martha Plimpton (to Keanu Reeves), *Parenthood*

209.

Fools aren't born, Pongo. Pretty girls make them in their spare time.

-- Jeff Daniels, *101 Dalmations*

210.

Why is life worth living? It's a very good question. Um ... Well, there are certain things, I guess, that make it worthwhile. Uh ... like what? Okay ... um ... For me, uh ... ooh ... I would say ... what, Groucho Marx, to name one thing ... uh ...um ... and Willie Mays ... and um ... the second movement of the Jupiter Symphony ... and um ... Louis Armstrong recording of *Potato Head Blues* ... um ... Swedish movies, naturally ... *Sentimental Education* by Flaubert ... uh... Marlon Brando, Frank Sinatra ... um ... those incredible apples and pears by Cezanne ... uh ... the crabs at Sam Wo's ... uh ... Tracy's face...

-- Woody Allen, *Manhattan*

211.

You shoot me in a dream, you better wake up and apologise.

-- Harvey Keitel, *Reservoir Dogs*

212.

Emily, I have a confession to make. I really am a horse doctor. But marry me, and I'll never look at another horse.

-- Groucho Marx, *A Day at the Races*
(last lines)

213.

Get up, boy. I bet you can squeal. I bet you can squeal like a pig.

-- Bill McKinney, *Deliverance*

214.

Get your stinkin' paws off me, you damn dirty ape!

-- Charlton Heston, *Planet of the Apes*

215.

Insanity runs in my family ... it practically gallops.

-- Cary Grant, *Arsenic and Old Lace*

216.

As far back as I can remember, I always wanted to be a gangster.

-- Ray Liotta, *Goodfellas*
(opening line)

217.

The last time I was this naked in public I was coming out of a uterus.

-- Sandra Bullock, *Miss Congeniality*

218.

I am not only walking out on this case, Mr Whiteside, I am leaving the nursing profession. I became a nurse because all my life, ever since I was a little girl, I was filled with the idea of serving a suffering humanity. After one month with you, Mr. Whiteside, I am going to work in a munitions factory. From now on, anything I can do to help exterminate the human race will fill me with the greatest of pleasure. If Florence Nightingale had ever nursed YOU, Mr Whiteside, she would have married Jack the Ripper instead of founding the Red Cross!

-- Mary Wickes, *The Man Who Came to Dinner*

219.

Wait a minute, wait a minute, you ain't heard nothing yet. Wait a minute, I've said, you ain't heard nothing yet. Wanna hear 'Toot, Toot, Tootsie'?

-- Al Jolson, *The Jazz Singer*
(the first lines ever spoken in film)

220.

Shoot straight ya bastards! Don't make a mess of it.

-- Edward Woodward, *'Breaker' Morant*
(last lines)

221.

Do you know how easily I could kill you, Frank? Do you know how many times I watched you go in and out of that bar? You are still alive because I have allowed you to live, so you show me some GODDAMN RESPECT!

-- John Malkovich, *In the Line of Fire*

222.

Whatever became of the moment when one first knew about death? There must have been one—a moment—in childhood, when it first occurred to you that you don't go on forever. It must have been shattering, stamped into one's memory. And yet, I can't remember it.

-- Gary Oldman, *Rosencrantz and Guildenstern Are Dead*

223.

Remember where you are—this is Thunderdome, and death is listening and will take the first man that screams.

-- Tina Turner, *Mad Max Beyond Thunderdome*

224.
That'll be the day.

-- John Wayne, *The Searchers*
(repeated line)

225.
A relationship, I think, is like a shark. You know? It has to constantly move forward or it dies. And I think what we got on our hands is a dead shark.

-- Woody Allen, *Annie Hall*

226.
Extraordinary! On the page it looked nothing. The beginning simple, almost comic. Just a pulse—bassoons and basset horns, like a rusty squeezebox. Then suddenly, high above it, an oboe, a single note, hanging there unwavering, till a clarinet took over and sweetened it into a phrase of such delight. This was no composition by a performing monkey! This was a music I'd never heard. Filled with such longing, such unfulfillable longing, it had me trembling. It seemed to me that I was hearing the voice of God.

-- F Murray Abraham, *Amadeus*

227.
'Course I'm respectable. I'm old. Politicians, ugly buildings and whores all get respectable if they last long enough.

-- John Huston, *Chinatown*

228.
I probably shan't return before dawn. How I detest dawn. The grass looks like it has been left out all night.

-- Clifton Webb, *The Dark Corner*

229.

Oh, it's the meek! 'Blessed are the *meek.*' Oh that's nice isn't it, because they get such an awful time.

      -- Carol Cleveland, *Life of Brian*

230.

I can't listen to that much Wagner, you know? I start to get the urge to conquer Poland.

      -- Woody Allen, *Manhattan Murder Mystery*

231.

I can't go all my life waiting to catch you between husbands.

      -- Clark Gable, *Gone With the Wind*

232.

They made us too smart, too quick, and too many. We are suffering for the mistakes they made because when the end comes, all that will be left ... is us.

      -- Jude Law (as a robot), *Artificial Intelligence: A.I.*

233.

Well, I like privacy when I retire. Yes, I'm very delicate in that respect. Prying eyes annoy me ... Behold the walls of Jericho! Uh, maybe not as thick as the ones that Joshua blew down with his trumpet, but a lot safer. You see, I have no trumpet.

      -- Clark Gable, *It Happened One Night*
(said while hoisting a bedsheet over a hotel-room clothesline between the two single beds where he and Claudette Colbert will be sleeping)

234.
In the navy there are four ways to do things: your way, the right way, the navy way and my way. You do things my way and we'll get along just fine.
-- Humphrey Bogart, *The Caine Mutiny*

235.
It's a very tiny country. Rhode Island could beat the crap out of it in a war … It costs sixty-five cents in a cab to go from one end of the island to the other. This is *not* a big place. They recently had the whole country carpeted. I'm talking small!
-- Dudley Moore, *Arthur*

236.
Oh no, it wasn't the airplanes. It was beauty killed the beast.
-- Robert Armstrong, *King Kong*
(last lines)

237.
By what you preach, none. But what that Comanche believes, ain't got no eyes … can't enter the spirit land … has to wander forever between the winds. You get it, Reverend?
-- John Wayne, *The Searchers*
(reasoning to the preacher why he just shot the eyes from a dead Comanche)

238.
Nothing is written.
-- Peter O'Toole, *Lawrence of Arabia*

239.

And the last thing he said to me, 'Rock,' he said, 'sometime when the team is up against it and the breaks are beating the boys, tell them to go out there with all they've got and win just one for the Gipper. I don't know where I'll be then, Rock,' he said, 'but I'll know about it and I'll be happy.'

-- Pat O'Brien, *Knute Rockne: All American*
(about Ronald Reagan's character)

240.

You want free speech? Let's see you acknowledge a man whose words make your blood boil who is standing centre-stage advocating at the top of his lungs that which you would spend a lifetime opposing at the top of yours.

-- Michael Douglas, *The American President*

241.

Peachy, I'm heartily ashamed for getting you killed instead of going home rich like you deserve to on account of me being so bleedin' high and bloody mighty. Can you forgive me?

-- Sean Connery, *The Man Who Would be King*
(to Michael Caine)

242.

We are from different worlds, you and me, Andrew. In mine, there was no time for bright fancies and happy inventions; no stopping for tea. The only game we played was to survive or go to war. If you didn't win, you just didn't finish. Loser, lose all. You probably don't understand that.

-- Michael Caine, *Sleuth*
(to Laurence Olivier)

243.

On the morning of his execution, King Charles the First put on two shirts. 'If I tremble with the cold,' he said, 'my enemies will say it was from fear. I will not expose myself to such reproaches.' We must also attempt this dignity as you mount the scaffold.

-- Laurence Olivier, *Sleuth*
(to Michael Caine)

244.

Well, how long is your program? Well, it was a million tiny little things that, when you added them all up, they meant we were supposed to be together ... and I knew it. I knew it the very first time I touched her. It was like coming home, only to no home I'd ever known. I was just taking her hand to help her out of a car and I knew. It was like ... magic.

-- Tom Hanks, *Sleepless in Seattle*

245.

Oh, cut the bleeding heart crap, will ya? We've all got our switches, lights, and knobs to deal with, Striker. I mean, down here there are literally hundreds and thousands of blinking, beeping, and flashing lights, blinking and beeping and flashing—they're *flashing* and they're *beeping*. I can't stand it anymore! They're BLINKING and *BEEPING* and *FLASHING!* Why doesn't somebody pull the plug?

-- William Shatner, *Flying High II*

246.

You can't shoot me! I have a very low threshold of death. My doctor says I can't have bullets enter my body at any time.

-- Woody Allen, *Casino Royale*

247.

'When Alexander saw the breadth of his domain, he wept, for there were no more worlds to conquer'. Benefits of a classical education.

-- Alan Rickman, *Die Hard*

248.

If I'd a been a ranch, they'd have named me the Bar Nothing.

-- Rita Hayworth, *Gilda*

249.

I used to live like Robinson Crusoe, shipwrecked among eight million people. Then one day I saw a footprint in the sand, and there you were.

-- Jack Lemmon, *The Apartment*

250.

You're television incarnate, Diana, indifferent to suffering, insensitive to joy. All of life reduced to the common rubble of banality. War, murder, death—all the same to you as bottles of beer, and the daily business of life is a corrupt comedy. You even shatter the sensations of time and space into split seconds and instant replays. You're madness, Diana.

-- William Holden, *Network*

251.

Time! Time. What is time? The Swiss manufacture it. The French hoard it. The Italians want it. Americans say it is money. Hindus say it does not exist. Do you know what I say? I say time is a crook.

-- Peter Lorre, *Beat the Devil*

252.

I get goose pimples. Even my goose pimples have goose pimples.

-- Bob Hope, *The Cat and the Canary*

253.
Casting me adrift 3,500 miles from a port of call? You're sending me to my doom, eh? Well you're wrong, Christian. I'll take this boat, as she floats, to England if I must. I'll live to see you—all of you—hanging from the highest yardarm in the British fleet.

-- Charles Laughton, *Mutiny on the Bounty*

254.
If I could get back my youth, I'd do anything in the world—except get up early, take exercise or be respectable.

-- George Sanders, *The Picture of Dorian Gray*

255.
Mr President, I'm not saying we wouldn't get our hair mussed. But I do say no more than ten to twenty million killed, tops. Uh, depending on the breaks.

-- George C Scott, *Dr Strangelove*

256.
Every time you hear a bell ring, it means an angel has just got its wings.

-- Henry Travers, *It's a Wonderful Life*

257.
It took more than one man to change my name to Shanghai Lily.

-- Marlene Dietrich, *Shanghai Express*

258.
There is no life, my darling, until you love and have been loved. And then there is no death.

-- Jennifer Jones, *Portrait of Jennie*

259.

We're on a mission from God.

-- Dan Aykroyd, *The Blues Brothers*

260.

Don't tell me how you are, Sherry. I want none of the tiresome details. I have very little time, and so the conversation shall be entirely about me, and I shall love it. Shall I tell you how I glittered through the South Seas like a silver scimitar? Or would you rather hear how I finished a three-act play with one hand and made love to the Maharajah's daughter with the other?

-- Reginald Gardiner, *The Man Who Came to Dinner* (in a take-off of Noel Coward)

261.

It's lavish, but I call it home.

-- Clifton Webb, *Laura*

262.

You're going to the cemetery with your toothbrush? How Egyptian.

-- Robin Williams, *The Birdcage*

263.

I'd just helped Ed Hickey into a taxi. Ed had been mixing his drinks and I felt he needed conveying. I started to walk down the street when I heard a voice saying, 'Good evening, Mr Dowd.' I turned, and there was this big white rabbit leaning against a lamppost. Well, I thought nothing of that. Because when you've lived in a town as long as I've lived in this one, you get used to the fact that everyone knows your name.

-- James Stewart, *Harvey*

264.

Live fast, die young and make a good-looking corpse.

-- John Derek, *Knock on Any Door*

265.

As God is my witness, as God is my witness they're not going to lick me!
I'm going to live through this and when it's all over, I'll never be hungry
again! No. Nor any of my folk. If I have to lie, steal, cheat or kill! As God is
my witness, I'll never be hungry again!

-- Vivien Leigh, *Gone With the Wind*

266.

Gentlemen, you can't fight in here! This is the War Room.

-- Peter Sellers, *Dr Strangelove*

267.

I apologise for the intelligence of my remarks, Sir Thomas. I had forgotten
that you were a member of Parliament.

-- George Sanders, *The Picture of Dorian Gray*

268.

I know I fib a good deal. After all, a woman's charm is fifty per cent illusion.

-- Vivien Leigh, *A Streetcar Named Desire*

269.

Well, this is where you came in, back at that pool again, the one I always
wanted. It's dawn now and they must have photographed me a thousand
times. Then they got a couple of pruning hooks from the garden and fished
me out ... ever so gently. Funny, how gentle people get with you once you're
dead.

-- William Holden, *Sunset Blvd.*

270.

I thought all writers drank to excess and beat their wives. You know, one time I secretly wanted to be a writer.

-- Cary Grant, *The Philadelphia Story*

271.

It's injustice I hate, not the Normans.

-- Errol Flynn, *The Adventures of Robin Hood*

272.

It was you, Fredo. I know it was you. You broke my heart. You broke my heart.

-- Al Pacino, *The Godfather Part II*

273.

Do I make you horny? Randy? Do I make you horny, baby, yeah, do I?

-- Mike Myers, *Austin Powers: International Man of Mystery*

274.

Someday, and that day may never come, I'll call upon you to do a service for me. But until that day, accept this justice as a gift on my daughter's wedding day.

-- Marlon Brando, *The Godfather*

275.

A condom is the glass slipper for our generation. You slip one on when you meet a stranger. You 'dance' all night, and then you throw it away.

-- Helena Bonham Carter, *Fight Club*

276.

That's my boy: always put one in the skull.

-- Kenny Graham, *Chopper*

277.

Everything begins and ends at exactly the right time and place.

-- Anne-Louise Lambert, *Picnic at Hanging Rock*

278.

The blues are because you're getting fat or it's been raining too long. You're just sad, that's all. The mean reds are horrible. Suddenly you're afraid, and you don't know what you're afraid of. Don't you ever get that feeling?

-- Audrey Hepburn, *Breakfast at Tiffany's*

279.

Remember, men, we're fighting for this woman's honour; which is probably more than she ever did.

-- Groucho Marx, *Duck Soup*

280.

Innocent? Is that supposed to be funny? An obese man, a disgusting man who could barely stand up; a man who if you saw him on the street, you'd point him out to your friends so that they could join you in mocking him; a man who, if you saw him while you were eating, you wouldn't be able to finish your meal ... After him, I picked the lawyer and I know you both must have been secretly thanking me for that one. This is a man who dedicated his life to making money by lying with every breath that he could muster to keeping murderers and rapists on the streets. A woman ... so ugly on the inside she couldn't bear to go on living if she couldn't be beautiful

74

on the outside. A drug dealer, a drug dealing pederast, actually. And let's not forget the disease-spreading whore. Only in a world this shitty could you even try to say these were innocent people and keep a straight face. But that's the point. We see a deadly sin on every street corner, in every home, and we tolerate it. We tolerate it because it's common, it's trivial. We tolerate it morning, noon and night. Well, not anymore. I'm setting the example. What I've done is going to be puzzled over and studied and followed ... forever.

-- Kevin Spacey, *Se7en*

281.
You see how picky I am about my shoes and they only go on my feet.

-- Alicia Silverstone, *Clueless*
(about her virginity)

282.
Alright. Alright, twenty something-betters. Uh, here goes. Uh, start with, uh, obvious: Excuse me, is that your nose or did a bus park on your face? Meteorological: Everybody take cover, she's going to BLOW! Fashionable: You know, you could de-emphasise your nose if you wore something larger—like Wyoming. Personal: Well, here we are, just the three of us. Punctual: Alright Delmond, your nose was on time, but you were fifteen minutes late! Envious: Ooh, I wish I was you. Gosh, to be able to smell your own ear. Naughty: Uh, pardon me, sir, some of the ladies have asked if you wouldn't mind putting that thing away. Philosophical: You know, it's not the size of a nose that's important, it's what's in it that matters. Humorous: Laugh, and the world laughs with you—sneeze, and it's goodbye Seattle! Commercial: Hi, I'm Earl Shive and I can paint that nose for thirty-nine, ninety-five! Polite: Uh, would you mind not bobbing your head, the, uh, orchestra keeps changing tempo. Melodic: Everybody... He's got the whole world *[Everyone singing along]* in his nose! Sympathetic: Aw, what happened, did your parents lose a bet with God? Complimentary: You must *love* the little birdies to give them this to perch on. Scientific: Say, does

that thing there influence the tides? Obscure: Whoof, I'd hate to see the grindstone … Think about it. Inquiring: When you stop to smell the flowers, are they afraid? French: Say, the pigs have refused to find any more truffles until you leave! Pornographic: Finally, a man who can satisfy two women at once! How many is that? Alright, alright. Religious: The Lord giveth, and he just kept on giving, didn't he? Disgusting: Say, who mows your nose hair? Ah, paranoid: Keep that guy away from my cocaine! Aromatic: It must be wonderful to wake up and smell the coffee … in Brazil. Appreciative: Ooh, how original. Most people just have their teeth capped. Alright, uh, alright. Dirty: Your name wouldn't be DICK, would it?

-- Steve Martin, *Roxanne*

(after he is asked for 20 insults about his own large nose)

283.

Heeeeere's Johnny!

-- Jack Nicholson, *The Shining*

284.

I've often speculated on why you don't return to America. Did you abscond with the church funds? Did you run off with a senator's wife? I like to think you killed a man. It's the romantic in me.

-- Claude Rains, *Casablanca*

285.

A policeman's job is only easy in a police state.

-- Charlton Heston, *Touch of Evil*

286.

The first rule of Fight Club is you do not talk about Fight Club. The second rule of Fight Club is: you DO NOT talk about Fight Club! Third rule of Fight Club: someone yells 'Stop!', goes limp, taps out, the fight is over. Fourth rule: only two guys to a fight. Fifth rule: one fight at a time, fellas. Sixth rule: no shirt, no shoes. Seventh rule: fights will go on as long as they have to. And the eighth and final rule: if this is your first night at Fight Club, you *have* to fight.

-- Brad Pitt, *Fight Club*

287.
We have ways of making men talk.

-- Douglass Dumbrille, *The Lives of a Bengal Lancer*

288.
Sports make you grunt and smell. Stay in school. Use your brains. Be a thinker, not a stinker.

-- Carl Weathers, *Rocky*

289.
Do you realise that in addition to fluoridating water, why, there are studies underway to fluoridate salt, flour, fruit juices, soup, sugar, milk, ice-cream? Ice-cream, Mandrake? Children's ice-cream! You know when fluoridation began? 1946. 1946, Mandrake. How does that coincide with your post-war Commie conspiracy, huh? It's incredibly obvious, isn't it? A foreign substance is introduced into our precious bodily fluids without the knowledge of the individual, and certainly without any choice. That's the way your hard-core Commie works. I first became aware of it, Mandrake, during the physical act of love ... Yes, a profound sense of fatigue, a feeling of emptiness followed. Luckily I was able to interpret these feelings correctly: loss of essence. I can assure you it has not recurred, Mandrake. Women ... women sense my power, and they seek the life essence. I do not avoid women, Mandrake, but I do deny them my essence.

-- Sterling Hayden, *Dr Strangelove*

290.

Woman can change better than a man. Man lives in jerks. Baby born or somebody dies, that's a jerk; gets a farm, or loses one, an' that's a jerk. With a woman, it's all one flow, like a stream, little eddies, little waterfalls, but the river it goes right on. Woman looks at it like that.

-- Jane Darwell, *The Grapes of Wrath*

291.

This never happened to the other fellow.

-- George Lazenby, *On Her Majesty's Secret Service*

292.

I'll make him an offer he can't refuse.

-- Al Pacino, *The Godfather*

293.

If you look around the table and you can't tell who the sucker is, it's you.

-- Paul Scofield, *Quiz Show*

294.

I'll hit you so hard, I'll kill your whole family.

-- Timothy Daly, *Diner*

295.

Whatever life holds in store for me, I will never forget these words: 'With great power comes great responsibility.' This is my gift; my curse. Who am I ...?

-- Tobey Maguire, *Spider-Man*

296.

Give me some death!

-- Val Kilmer (as Jim Morrision), *The Doors*

297.

My name is Inigo Montoya. You killed my father. Prepare to die!

-- Mandy Patinkin, *The Princess Bride*

(repeated line)

298.

Please, sir, I want some more.'

-- Mark Lester, *Oliver!*

299.

I'd be unworthy of the high trust that's been placed in me if I didn't do everything in my power to keep our beloved Freedonia in peace with the world. I'd be only too happy to meet with Ambassador Trentino, and offer him on behalf of my country the right hand of good fellowship. And I feel sure he will accept this gesture in the spirit of which it is offered. But suppose he doesn't. A fine thing that'll be. I hold out my hand and he refuses to accept. That'll add a lot to my prestige, won't it? Me, the head of a country, snubbed by a foreign ambassador. Who does he think he is, that he can come here, and make a sap of me in front of all my people? Think of it—I hold out my hand and that hyena refuses to accept. Why, the cheap ball-pushing swine, he'll never get away with it I tell you, he'll never get away with it! *[Trentino enters]* So, you refuse to shake hands with me, eh? *[He slaps Trentino and the war is on.]*

-- Groucho Marx, *Duck Soup*

300.

You don't make up for your sins in church. You do it in the streets. You do it at home. The rest is bullshit and you know it.

-- Martin Scorcese, *Mean Streets*
(opening voice-over)

301.

You're gonna eat lightnin' and you're gonna crap thunder!

-- Burgess Meredith, *Rocky*

302.

You will never find a more wretched hive of scum and villainy. We must be cautious.

-- Alec Guinness, *Star Wars*

303.

Oh, that's the first sane remark I've heard today. C'm'along, Dexter, I know a formula that's said to pop the pennies off the eyelids of dead Irishmen.

-- Roland Young, *The Philadelphia Story*

304.

I've seen things you people wouldn't believe. Attack ships on fire off the shoulder of Orion. I watched C-beams glitter in the dark near the Tannhauser Gate. All those moments will be lost in time, like tears in rain. Time to die.

-- Rutger Hauer, *Blade Runner*

305.

I've met another man. He's the best man I've ever met. He's bright, handsome and he's crazy about me. And he's married. There's only one thing: he doesn't like my hat.

-- Lena Olin, *The Unbearable Lightness of Being*

306.

It shrinks my liver, doesn't it, Nat? It pickles my kidneys, yeah. But what it does to the mind ... It tosses the sandbags overboard so the balloon can soar. Suddenly I'm above the ordinary. I'm competent. I'm walking a tightrope over Niagara Falls. I'm one of the great ones. I'm Michelangelo, moulding the beard of Moses. I'm Van Gogh, painting pure sunlight. I'm Horowitz, playing the Emperor Concerto. I'm John Barrymore before movies got him by the throat. I'm Jesse James and his two brothers, all three of them. I'm William Shakespeare. And out there it's not Third Avenue any longer, it's the Nile. Nat, it's the Nile and down it moves the barge of Cleopatra.

-- Ray Milland, *The Lost Weekend*
(about alcoholism)

307.

Me and God, we'd be mates.

-- Paul Hogan, *Crocodile Dundee*

308.

I made Louis take me on Crusade. I dressed my women as Amazons and we rode bare-breasted halfway to Damascus. Louis had a seizure and I damn near died of windburn... but the troops were dazzled.

-- Katharine Hepburn, *The Lion in Winter*
(as Eleanor of Aquitaine)

309.

Missing? Please! It's the weekend. He's most likely holed up in some hotel somewhere with a girl. Or a guy ... farm animal ... whatever. Weren't you ever eighteen?

-- John Neville, *Urban Legend*

310.
Uh, well, sir, I ain't a f'real cowboy. But I am one helluva stud!

-- Jon Voight, *Midnight Cowboy*

311.
The difference between a lady and a flower girl is not how she behaves, but how she is treated.

-- Audrey Hepburn, *My Fair Lady*

312.
There are two kinds of people in this world: Those that enter a room and turn the television set on, and those that enter a room and turn the television set off.

-- Lawrence Harvey, *The Manchurian Candidate*

313.
Young men make wars, and the virtues of war are the virtues of young men: courage and hope for the future. Then old men make the peace, and the vices of peace are the vices of old men: mistrust and caution.

-- Alec Guinness, *Lawrence of Arabia*

314.
Your fugitive's name is *Doctor* Richard Kimble. What I want out of everyone of you is a hard-target search, of every gas station, residence, warehouse, farmhouse, henhouse, outhouse and doghouse in that area!

-- Tommy Lee Jones, *The Fugitive*

315.

Terminate with extreme prejudice.

-- Jerry Ziesmer, *Apocalypse Now*

316.

I'm bigger than you and higher up the food chain ... so get in my belly!

-- Mike Myers, *Austin Powers: The Spy Who Shagged Me*
(as Fat Bastard)

317.

Well that's great, that's just fuckin' great, man, now what the fuck are we supposed to do? We're in some real pretty shit now, man ... That's it, man, game over, man, game over, man! Game over!

-- Bill Paxton, *Aliens*

318.

Wanna know how I got these scars? My father was a drinker. And a fiend. And one night he goes off crazier than usual. Mummy gets the kitchen knife to defend herself. He doesn't like that. Not one bit. So, me watching, he takes the knife to her, laughing while he does it. Turns to me and he says, 'Why so serious, son?' Comes at me with the knife ... 'Why so serious?' He sticks the blade in my mouth ... 'Let's put a smile on that face!' And ... why so serious?

-- Heath Ledger, *The Dark Knight*

319.

By the cut of your suit, you went to Oxford or wherever. Naturally, you think human beings dress like that. But you wear it with such disdain, my guess is you didn't come from money, and your school friends never let you forget it. Which means that you were at that school by the grace of someone else's charity, hence that chip on your shoulder. And since your first thought about me ran to 'orphan', that's what I'd say you are—oh, you are? I like this poker thing. And that makes perfect sense! Since MI6 looks for maladjusted young men who give little thought to sacrificing others in order to protect queen and country. You know, former SAS types with easy smiles and expensive watches. Rolex?

-- Eva Green, *Casino Royale* (2006)

320.

Bullshit! I know Nixon personally. He lugs a trainload of shit behind him that could fertilise the Sinai. Why, I wouldn't buy an apple from the son of a bitch and I consider him a good, close, personal friend.

-- Noble Willingham, *Good Morning Vietnam*
(As the General, responding to JT Walsh's outrage over an off-the-wall comment about Nixon made by Robin Williams on the air)

321.
Death is ... whimsical ... today.

-- Gary Oldman, *Leon (aka The Professional)*

322.
I believe in America. America has made my fortune.

-- Salvatore Corsitto, *The Godfather*

323.
What, you don't think I know how to get myself off? Hell, that's what half of band camp is: sex-ed! So, are we gonna screw soon? 'Cause I'm getting kinda antsy.

-- Alyson Hannigan, *American Pie*
(explaining her unconventional use of a flute in band camp)

324.

Your man Christian is a cake boy. He's a disco-dancin', Oscar Wilde-readin', Streisand ticket-holdin' friend of Dorothy, know what I'm sayin'?

-- Donald Faison, *Clueless*

325.

Let her go or die, that's the only choice you got to make!

-- Sidney Poitier, *Shoot to Kill* (aka *Deadly Pursuit*)

326.

I'm not a Roman, mum. I'm a kike, a yid, a heebie, a hook-nose. I'm kosher, mum. I'm a Red Sea pedestrian and proud of it!

-- Graham Chapman, *Life of Brian*

327.

Just when I thought I was out, they pull me back in!

-- Al Pacino, *The Godfather Part III*

328.

By the authority vested in me by Kaiser Wilhelm the Second, I pronounce you husband and wife. Proceed with the execution.

-- Peter Bull, *The African Queen*

329.

Hey, STELLAAAAHH!

-- Marlon Brando, *A Streetcar Named Desire*

330.

I'm just writing the report now. We haven't quite decided whether he committed suicide or died trying to escape.

-- Claude Rains, *Casablanca*

331.
I have become a virgin.

·· Cate Blanchett, *Elizabeth*

332.
Bridget Jones, wanton sex goddess with a very bad man between her thighs ... Mum! Hi!

·· Renee Zellweger, *Bridget Jones' Diary*
(on the phone)

333.
I'm going to be a great film star! That is, if booze and sex don't get me first.

·· Liza Minnelli, *Cabaret*

334.
Women need a reason for having sex. Men just need a place.

·· Billy Crystal, *City Slickers*

335.
Don't get mad. Get everything.

·· Ivana Trump, *First Wives Club*

336.
One Rocco more or less isn't worth dying for.

·· Humphrey Bogart, *Key Largo*

337.
What change is there in me? Egyptian or Hebrew, I am still Moses. These are the same hands, the same arms, the same face that were mine a moment ago.

·· Charlton Heston, *The Ten Commandments*

338.

Give me the child. Through dangers untold and hardships unnumbered, I have fought my way here to the castle beyond the goblin city to take back the child that you have stolen, for my will is as strong as yours, and my kingdom is as great. You have no power over me.

-- Jennifer Connelly, *Labyrinth*

339.

You are one... ugly... motherfucker.

-- Arnold Schwarzenegger, *Predator*

340.

How DARE you and the rest of your barbarians set fire to my library! Play conqueror all you want, mighty Caesar! Rape, murder, pillage thousands, even millions, of human beings. But neither you nor any other barbarian has the right to destroy *one* human thought!

-- Elizabeth Taylor, *Cleopatra*

341.

Rosebud.

-- Orson Welles, *Citizen Kane*

342.

Pining? Men don't pine. Girls pine. Men just ... suffer.

-- Fred Astaire, *The Gay Divorcee*

343.

Is this your wife? What a lovely throat.

-- Max Shreck, *Nosferatu*

344.

Dear fellow countrymen, just a few words to let you know that this story is going to be all about me. So, in answer to many requests, here is the story of my career ... Here is the story, of my career ... my brilliant career. I make no apologies for sounding egotistical ... because I am!

-- Judy Davis, *My Brilliant Career*

345.

No wire hangers! What's wire hangers doing in this closet when I told you no wire hangers?! EVER!

-- Faye Dunaway, *Mommie Dearest*
(as Joan Crawford)

346.

You just fulfilled the first rule of law enforcement: make sure when your shift is over, you go home alive. Here endeth the lesson.

-- Sean Connery, *The Untouchables*

347.

Oh, he's just like any other man, only more so.

-- Humphrey Bogart, *Casablanca*
(about Claude Rains)

348.

Good riddance to bad rubbish!

-- Bette Davis, *Of Human Bondage*

349.

Never a man made sound, and then ... Mozart.

-- Robert Redford, *Out of Africa*

350.

You know, when they forced Khruschev out, he sat down and wrote two letters to his successor. He said, 'When you get yourself into a situation you can't get out of, open the first letter, and you'll be safe. When you get yourself into another situation you can't get out of, open the second letter.' Soon enough, he gets into a tight situation, and he opens the first letter. It says, 'Blame it all on me'. So he blames it all on the old guy, and it worked like a charm. When he got himself into a second situation, he opened the second letter. It said, 'Sit down, and write two letters...'

-- James Brolin, *Traffic*

351.

A little advice about feelings, kiddo: don't expect it always to tickle.

-- Judd Hirsch, *Ordinary People*

352.

Today is a good day to die.

-- Chief Dan George, *Little Big Man*
(and later, Keifer Sutherland, *Flatliners*)

353.

My dear, life rarely gives us what we want at the moment we consider appropriate. Adventures do occur, but not punctually.

-- Peggy Ashcroft, *A Passage to India*

354.

Sun is bad for you. Everything our parents said was good is bad: sun, milk, red meat ... college.

-- Woody Allen, *Annie Hall*

355.

I've always thought a good lashing with a buggy whip would benefit you immensely.

-- Clark Gable, *Gone With the Wind*

356.

Mind if I smoke while you're eating?

-- Dolly Sharp, *Deep Throat*

357.

Stop it! Stop it! Stop it right now! Stop it! Alright, no one is to stone anyone until I blow this whistle. Even—and I want to make this absolutely clear— even if they do say, 'Jehovah'. *[A giant boulder lands on his head.]*

-- John Cleese, *Life of Brian*

358.

General Kenobi, years ago you served my father in the Clone Wars ... now he begs you to help him in his struggle against the Empire. I regret that I am unable to present my father's request to you in person. But my ship has fallen under attack and I'm afraid my mission to Alderaan has failed. I've placed information vital to the survival of the rebellion into the memory systems of this R2 unit. My father will know how to retrieve it. You must see this droid safely delivered to him on Alderaan. This is our most desperate hour. Help me, Obi-Wan Kenobi. You're my only hope.

-- Carrie Fisher, *Star Wars*

359.

Why should I love God? He strung up his only son like a side of veal. I shudder to think what he'd do to me.

-- Geoffrey Rush, *Quills*
(as Marquis de Sade)

360.

It's life, Captain, but not life as we know it.

-- Leonard Nimoy, *Star Trek: The Motion Picture*

361.

I'm pretty sure there's a lot more to life than being really, really good looking. And I plan on finding out what that is.

-- Ben Stiller, *Zoolander*

362.

What's your favourite scary movie?

-- Roger Jackson, *Scream*
(on the phone to Drew Barrymore)

363.

My teenage angst bullshit now has a body count.

-- Winona Ryder, *Heathers*

364.

I think someone should just take this city and just ... just flush it down the fuckin' toilet.

-- Robert De Niro, *Taxi Driver*

365.

Mother is the name for God on the lips and hearts of all children. Your daughter is out there on the streets waiting for you.

-- Brandon Lee, *The Crow*

366.

Get out! Go anywhere you want. Go to a hotel. Go live with her, and don't come back! Because after twenty five years of building a home and raising a family and all the senseless pain that we have inflicted on each other, I'm damned if I'm going to stand here and have you tell me you're in love with somebody else. Because this isn't a convention weekend with your secretary, is it? Or … or some broad that you picked up after three belts of booze. This is your great winter romance, isn't it? Your last roar of passion before you settle into your emeritus years. Is that what's left for me? Is that my share? She gets the winter passion, and I get the dotage? What am I supposed to do? Am I supposed to sit at home knitting and purling while you slink back like some penitent drunk? I'm your wife, damn it! And if you can't work up a winter passion for me, the least I require is respect and allegiance. I hurt. Don't you understand that? I hurt badly!

-- Beatrice Straight, *Network*
(She won an Oscar for this scene.)

367.

You are a sad, strange, little man. You have my pity. Farewell.

-- Tim Allen, *Toy Story*

368.

No! Try not. Do… or do not. There is no try.

-- Frank Oz, *The Empire Strikes Back*
(as Yoda)

369.

When I'm good, I'm very good. But when I'm bad, I'm better.

-- Mae West, *I'm No Angel*

370.

We rob banks.

.. Faye Dunaway, *Bonnie and Clyde*

371.

My evil self is at the door, and I have no power to stop it.

.. Walter Pidgeon, *Forbidden Planet*

372.

I'll have a half double-decaffeinated half-caf ... with a twist of lemon.

.. Steve Martin, *LA Story*

373.

You'd think the rain would've cooled things down. All it did was make the heat wet.

.. Thelma Ritter, *Rear Window*

374.

Do you have a valediction, boy-o?

.. James Cromwell, *LA Confidential*

375.

Would you mind NOT shooting at the thermonuclear weapons!

.. John Travolta, *Broken Arrow*

376.

You know, you, uh, ought to take a look at the statistics on suicide sometime. You might learn a little something about the insurance business. Come now, you've never read an actuarial table in your life, have you? Why, they've got ten volumes on suicide alone. Suicide by race, by colour, by occupation, by sex, by seasons of the year, by time of day. Suicide, how committed: by poisons, by firearms, by drowning, by leaps. Suicide by poison, subdivided by types of poison, such as corrosive, irritant, systemic, gaseous, narcotic, alkaloid, protein, and so forth. Suicide by leaps, subdivided by leaps from high places, under the wheels of trains, under the wheels of trucks, under the feet of horses, from steamboats. But Mr Norton, of all the cases on record, there's not one single case of suicide by leap from the rear end of a moving train. And do you know how fast that train was going at the point where the body was found? 15 miles an hour. Now, how can anybody jump off a slow-moving train like that with any kind of expectation that he would kill himself? No, no soap, Mr. Norton. We're sunk and we'll have to pay through the nose, and you know it.

-- Edward G Robinson, *Double Indemnity*

377.

And crawling on this planet's face, some insects called the human race. Lost in time. And lost in space...

-- Charles Gray, *Rocky Horror Picture Show*

378.

He doesn't understand the concept of money? He just inherited three million dollars and he doesn't understand the concept of money? Wow, good work, Dad. I'm getting fucking poetic here.

-- Tom Cruise, *Rain Man*

379.

This is supposed to be an 'appy occasion. Let's not bicker and argue about who killed who ...

-- Michael Palin, *Monty Python and the Holy Grail*

380.

It's not the years, honey. It's the mileage.

-- Harrison Ford, *Raiders of the Lost Ark*

381.

How much for the little girl? Your women—how much for the women?

-- John Belushi, *The Blues Brothers*

382.

Zihuatanejo.

-- Morgan Freeman, *The Shawshank Redemption*

383.

I'm tired of getting the fuzzy end of the lollipop.

-- Marilyn Monroe, *Some Like it Hot*

384.

This is your life and it's ending one minute at a time.

-- Edward Norton, *Fight Club*

385.

Aah, the serenity!

-- Michael Caton, *The Castle*

386.

I'll torture you so slowly, you'll think it's a career.

-- Richard E Grant, *Hudson Hawk*

387.

WHAT ... are you prepared ... to do!?

-- Sean Connery, *The Untouchables*

388.

There are children here somewhere. I can smell them.

-- Robert Helpmann, *Chitty Chitty Bang Bang*
(as the Child Catcher)

389.

If you want to call me that, smile.

-- Gary Cooper, *The Virginian*
(to Walter Huston, who was just about to call him a 'son-of-a—')

390.

I'll have what she's having.

-- Estelle Reiner (the director's mother), *When Harry Met Sally*

391.

**Keaton once said, 'I don't believe in God, but I'm afraid of him'. Well I
believe in God, and the only thing that scares me is Keyser Soze.**

-- Kevin Spacey, *The Usual Suspects*

392.

Well here's another nice mess you've gotten me into.

-- Oliver Hardy, *Another Fine Mess*

393.

**As my dear old grandfather Litvak said—just before they swung the trap—
he said, 'You can't cheat an honest man. Never give a sucker an even break,
or smarten up a chump'.**

-- WC Fields, *You Can't Cheat an Honest Man*

394.

Did you ever have the feeling that you wanted to go, and still have the feeling that you wanted to stay?

-- Jimmy Durante, *The Man Who Came to Dinner*

395.

Magic mirror on the wall, who's the fairest one of all?

-- Lucille La Verne, *Snow White and the Seven Dwarfs*

396.

I am big. It's the pictures that got small.

-- Gloria Swanson, *Sunset Blvd.*

397.

Right turn, Clyde.

-- Clint Eastwood, *Every Which Way But Loose*

398.

You're a very nosy fellow, kitty-cat, huh? You know what happens to nosy fellows? Huh, no? Want to guess? Huh, no? OK. They lose their noses.

-- Roman Polanski, *Chinatown*

399.

It's not the men in your life that count, it's the life in your men.

-- Mae West, *I'm No Angel*

400.

Where's the rest of me?

-- Ronald Reagan, *Kings Row*

401.
Pop quiz, hotshot: there's a bomb on a bus. Once the bus goes fifty miles an hour, the bomb is armed. If it drops below fifty, it blows up. What do you do? What do you do?

-- Dennis Hopper, *Speed*

402.
A good fight should be like a small play, but played seriously. When the opponent expands, I contract. When he contracts, I expand. And when the opportunity presents itself, I do not hit. It hits all by itself.

-- Bruce Lee, *Enter the Dragon*

403.
Now I want you to remember that no bastard ever won a war by dying for his country. He won it by making the other poor dumb bastard die for his country.

-- George C Scott, *Patton*

404.
This is going straight to the pool room.

-- Michael Caton, *The Castle*

405.
'Anything "I" say'...what a wonderful philosophy you have.

-- Hugh Keyes Byrne, *Mad Max*

406.
You unlock this door with the key of imagination. Beyond it is another dimension—a dimension of sound, a dimension of sight, a dimension of

mind. You're moving into a land of both shadow and substance, of things and ideas. You've just crossed over into the Twilight Zone.

-- Burgess Meredith, *Twilight Zone: The Movie*
(narrating)

407.
Hmm, death by mini-bar.

-- Rupert Everett, *My Best Friend's Wedding*

408.
Good mo-o-o-o-o-rnin' Vietnaaaaaam! Hey, this is not a test. This is rock'n'roll. Time to rock it from the delta to the DMZ!

-- Robin Williams, *Good Morning Vietnam*

409.
You aren't really anybody in America if you're not on TV.

-- Nicole Kidman, *To Die For*

410.
You want a leg or a breast?

-- Grace Kelly, *To Catch a Thief*

411.
Wait a minute! Wait. Wait. I'm having a thought. Oh yes. Oh yes. I'm going to have a thought. It's coming. It's coming ... It's gone.

-- Al Pacino, *Dick Tracy*

412.
Your small minds are muscle-bound with suspicion. That's because the only exercise you ever get is jumping to conclusions.

-- Danny Kaye, *The Secret Life of Walter Mitty*

413.
They call me MISTER Tibbs.

-- Sidney Poitier, *In the Heat of the Night*

414.
Dev, is that you? I am glad you are late. This chicken took longer than I expected ... Hope it isn't done too much ... Of course, it caught on fire once ... I think it is better that I cut it out here, unless you want half of one for yourself. We're going to have knives and forks, after all, I've decided we're going to eat in style ... Marriage must be wonderful with this sort of thing going on everyday.

-- Ingrid Bergman, *Notorious*

415.
You know, you've got the brain of a four-year old child, and I bet he was glad to get rid of it.

-- Groucho Marx, *Horse Feathers*

416.
And I guess that was your accomplice in the wood-chipper.

-- Frances McDormand, *Fargo*

417.
Well, if there's a bright centre to the universe, you're on the planet that it's farthest from.

-- Mark Hamill, *Star Wars*

418.
She tried to sit in my lap... while I was standing up.

-- Humphrey Bogart, *The Big Sleep*
(about Lauren Bacall)

419.

You're nuts to let a girl go that calls you Lotte. I tell you that as a friend.

-- Charlie Sheen, *Being John Malkovich*
(as himself, to John Malkovich)

420.

I'm hard to get, Steve. All you have to do is ask me.

-- Lauren Bacall, *To Have and Have Not*
(to Humphrey Bogart)

421.

Champagne for my real friends, and real pain for my sham friends.

-- Edward Norton, *The 25th Hour*

422.

There's only one proper way for a professional soldier to die: the last bullet of the last battle of the last war.

-- George C Scott, *Patton*

423.

Beulah, peel me a grape.

-- Mae West, *I'm No Angel*

424.

Wars, conflict—it's all business. One murder makes a villain; millions, a hero. Numbers sanctify!

-- Charles Chaplin, *Monsieur Verdoux*

425.

Lucius will stay with me now. And if his mother so much as looks at me in a manner that displeases me, he will die. If she decides to be noble, and takes her own life he will die. *[To his own sister]* And as for you, you will love me as I loved you. You will provide me with an heir of pure blood, so that Commodus and his progeny will rule for a thousand years. Am I not merciful? AM I NOT MERCIFUL?!

-- Joaquin Phoenix, *Gladiator*

426.

Where are you going? Oh, you men are all alike! Seven or eight quick ones and then you're out with the boys to boast and brag! YOU BETTER KEEP YOUR MOUTH SHUT! Oh... I think I love him.

-- Madeline Kahn, *Young Frankenstein*
(to the monster)

427.

You know the difference between you and me? I make this look good.

-- Will Smith, *Men in Black*
(to Tommy Lee Jones, about their uniforms)

428.

My father was a drunk, a gambler and a womaniser. I worshipped him.

-- John Travolta, *The General's Daughter*

429.

Remember George: no man is a failure who has friends.

-- Henry Travers, *It's a Wonderful Life*

430.

My mother thanks you. My father thanks you. My sister thanks you. And I thank you.

-- James Cagney, *Yankee Doodle Dandy*

431.

I never drink ... wine.

-- Gary Oldman, *Bram Stoker's Dracula*

432.

I wondered if a memory is something you have or something you've lost.

-- Gena Rowlands, *Another Woman*

433.

Jason was my son, and today is his birthday.

-- Betsy Palmer, *Friday the 13th*

434.

All of you! You all killed him! And my brother, and Riff. Not with bullets, or guns—with hate. Well now I can kill, too, because now I have hate!

-- Natalie Wood, *West Side Story*

435.

We look fabulous.

-- Guy Pearce, The Adventures of Priscilla: Queen of the Desert

436.

Shane! Come back!

-- Brandon De Wilde, *Shane*
(final lines)

437.
So they call me Concentration Camp Ehrhardt?

-- Jack Benny, *To Be or Not to Be*

438.
Commander, tear this ship apart until you've found those plans. And bring me the passengers. I want them alive!

-- James Earl Jones (voicing Darth Vader), *Star Wars*

439.
Kiss me. Kiss me as if it were the last time.

-- Ingrid Bergman, *Casablanca*

440.
You have chosen ... poorly.

-- Robert Eddison, *Indiana Jones and the Last Crusade*

441.
I feel as if I've travelled my whole life just to stand here.

-- John Hurt, *The Elephant Man*

442.
What do you know about it? Who are you, anyway? Who are you? Criminals? Are you proud of yourselves? Proud of breaking safes or cheating at cards? Things you could just as well keep your fingers off. You wouldn't need to do all that if you'd learn a proper trade or if you'd work. If you weren't a bunch of lazy bastards. But I ... I can't help myself! I have no control over this, this evil thing inside of me, the fire, the voices, the torment! It's there all the time, driving me out to wander the streets, following me, silently, but I can feel it there. It's me pursuing myself. I want

to escape, to escape from myself. But it's impossible. I can't escape, I have to obey it. I have to run, run … endless streets. I want to escape, to get away. And I'm pursued by ghosts. Ghosts of mothers and of those children … they never leave me. They are always there … always, always, always! Except when I do it, when I … Then I can't remember anything. And afterwards I see those posters and read what I've done, and read, and read … did I do that? But I can't remember anything about it. But who will believe me? Who knows what it's like to be me? How I'm forced to act … how I must, must … don't want to, must! Don't want to, but must! And then a voice screams. I can't bear to hear it. I can't go on! I can't … I can't …

-- Peter Lorre, *M*

443.
Instant gratification takes too long.

-- Meryl Streep, *Postcards from the Edge*

444.
Phil? Phil Connors? Phil Connors, I thought that was you. Now don't you tell me you don't remember me, 'cause I sure as heckfire remember you. Ned! Ryerson! 'Needlenose Ned'? 'Ned the Head'? C'mon, buddy, Case Western High. I did the whistling belly-button trick at the high school talent show? Bing! Ned Ryerson, got the shingles real bad senior year, almost didn't graduate? Bing, again! Ned Ryerson, I dated your sister Mary Pat a couple of times until you told me not to anymore. Well?

-- Stephen Tobolowsky, *Groundhog Day*

445.
Adrian! Adrian!

-- Sylvester Stallone, *Rocky*

446.

You know, Rick, I have many a friend in Casablanca, but somehow, just because you despise me, you are the only one I trust.

-- Peter Lorre, *Casablanca*

447.

For the same reason you are not: it was the way I was brought up.

-- George Voskovec, *12 Angry Men*
(to Ed Begley about why he is so polite)

448.

The only true currency in this bankrupt world ... is what you share with someone else when you're uncool.

-- Philip Seymour Hoffman, *Almost Famous*

449.

It's like my mother always said: 'Two tears in a bucket, motherfuck it!'

-- The Lady Chablis, *Midnight in the Garden of Good and Evil*
(as herself)

450.

James, earn this ... Earn it!

-- Tom Hanks, *Saving Private Ryan*

451.

The time to make up your mind about people is never.

-- Katharine Hepburn, *The Philadelphia Story*

452.

This you know: the years travel fast. And time after time I've done the Tell.
But this ain't one 'body's Tell. It's the Tell of us all. And you gotta listen it and
'member, 'cuz what you hears today, you gotta tell the newborn tomorrow.
I was lookin' behind us now, into history back. I see those of us that got the
luck and started the haul for home. And I 'members how it led us here and
how we was heartful 'cuz we'd seen what there once was. One look and we
knew we'd got it straight. Those who had gone before had the knowin' and
doin' of things beyond our reckonin'. Even beyond our dreamin'... Time
counts and keeps countin'. And we knows now, finding the trick of what's
being and lost ain't no easy ride. But that's our track. We gotta travel it and
there ain't nobody knows where it's gonna lead. Still, in all, every night
we does the Tell so that we 'member who we was and where we came
from. But most of all we 'members the man who finded us, him that came
the salvage. And we lights the city, not just for him, but for all of them that
are still out there, 'cuz we knows there'll come a night when they sees the
distant light, and they'll be comin' home.

-- Helen Buday, *Mad Max Beyond Thunderdome*
(to her adopted children, in the ruins of Sydney)

453.

Jimmy, do you like movies about gladiators?

-- Peter Graves, *Flying High II*

454.

The young ones make great pets. Just make sure you kill them before they
mature. Believe me, the last thing you want is a human teenager running
around your house.

-- Paul Giamatti, *Planet of the Apes* (1961)

455.

Jimmy, have you ever been to a Turkish prison?

-- Peter Graves, *Flying High II*

456.

Oh, Frank. My lips are hot. Kiss my hot lips.

-- Sally Kellerman, *MASH*

457.

You ever seen a grown man naked?

-- Peter Graves, *Flying High II*

458.

God gave men brains larger than dogs' so they wouldn't hump women's legs at cocktail parties.

-- Angelina Jolie, *Hackers*

459.

Saayyy, Scraps is a *boy* dog.

-- Peter Graves, *Flying High II*

460.

James Bond. You appear with the tedious inevitability of an unloved season.

-- Michael Lonsdale, *Moonraker*

461.

Woah!

-- Keanu Reeves, *The Matrix*

462.

I'll have a lemonade … in a dirty glass.

-- Bob Hope, *Road to Utopia*

463.

Five thousand of my men are out there in the freezing mud. Three thousand of them are bloody and cleaved. Two thousand will never leave this place. I will not believe they fought and died for nothing!

-- Russell Crowe, *Gladiator*

464.

I'll tell you what he said. He asked me to forcibly insert the Life Line exercise card into my anus.

-- Beth Grant, *Donnie Darko*

465.

Get the butter.

-- Marlon Brando, *Last Tango in Paris*

466.

Whenever I get gloomy with the state of the world, I think of the arrivals gate at Heathrow Airport. General opinion's starting to make out that we live in a world of hatred and greed, but I don't see that. It seems to me that love is everywhere. Often it's not particularly defined or newsworthy, but it's always there—fathers and sons, mothers and daughters, husbands and wives, boyfriends, girlfriends, old friends. When the planes hit the twin towers, as far as I know, none of the phone calls from people on board were messages of hate or revenge. They were all messages of love. And, if you look for it, I've got a sneaking suspicion that love, actually, is all around.

-- Hugh Grant, *Love, Actually*
(as the Prime Minister of Britain)

467.

To Theodore Roosevelt: you are like the wind, and I like the lion. You form the tempest. The sand stings my eyes and the ground is parched. I roar in defiance but you do not hear. But between us there is a difference. I, like the lion, must remain in my place. While you, like the wind, will never know yours. Mulay Hamid El Raisuli The Magnificent, Lord of the Riff, Sultan to the Berbers, Last of the Barbary Pirates.

-- Sean Connery, *The Wind and the Lion*

468.

I am the Third Revelation!

-- Daniel Day-Lewis, *There Will Be Blood*

469.

Well it's been one long, god-damned, hot, miserable, shit-ass fuckin' day every inch of the way.

-- Michael Parks, *From Dusk Till Dawn*

470.

They come here looking for the magic, hoping to find romance when they can't find it anywhere else. It's an island, babe. If you didn't bring it here, you won't find it here.

-- Harrison Ford, *Six Days, Seven Nights*

471.

I wish I knew how to quit you.

-- Jake Gyllenhaal, *Brokeback Mountain*

472.

Nobody puts Baby in the corner.

-- Patrick Swayze, *Dirty Dancing*

473.

Now, go do the voodoo that you do so well.

-- Harvey Korman, *Blazing Saddles*

474.

This is Ohio. I mean, if you don't have a brewski in your hand you might as well be wearing a dress.

-- Christian Slater, *Heathers*

475.

Here's something to remember when you're older, Thomas—never pass up a bathroom, never waste a hard-on, and never trust a fart.

-- Jack Nicholson, *The Bucket List*

476.

You know, I'm not the only one that changed when you came to East High. Kids that I just used to pass in the hallway, we're friends now, and we're supposed to be doing this show together. The problem is East High changed when you got there and now it's changed again because you left. You might be ready to say good bye to East High, but East High is not ready to say good bye to you.

-- Zac Efron, *High School Musical 3*

477.

I am the Earth Mother, and you are all flops.

-- Elizabeth Taylor, *Who's Afraid of Virginia Woolf?*

478.

Enough is enough! I have had it with these motherfucking snakes on this motherfucking plane!

-- Samuel L Jackson, *Snakes on a Plane*

479.

I'd like to kiss you, but I just washed my hair.

-- Bette Davis, *The Cabin in the Cotton*

480.

He's not gonna 'hit the streets', Jim. Thirty years ago he was a highly trained SAS operative. He is my age now, for Christ's sake. I have to get up three times a night to take a piss!

-- Philip Baker Hall, *The Rock*
(on the decision to release a serial escapee from prison)

481.

Son, you're about as useful as a cock-flavoured lollipop.

-- Rip Torn, *Dodgeball: A True Underdog Story*

482.

To infinity and beyond!

-- Tim Allen, *Toy Story*

483.

As the cars roar into Pennsylvania, the cradle of liberty, it seems apparent that our citizens are staying off the streets, which may make scoring particularly difficult, even with this year's rule changes. To recap those revisions: women are still worth ten points more than men in all age brackets, but teenagers now rack up forty points, and toddlers under

twelve now rate a big seventy points. The big score: anyone, any sex, over
75 years old has been upped to one hundred points.

-- Carle Bensen, Death Race 2000

484.

In my class, you will learn to think for yourselves again. You will learn
to savour words and language. No matter what anybody tells you, words
and ideas can change the world. I see that look in Mr Pitts' eyes like 19th
century literature has nothing to do with going to business school or
medical school, right? Maybe. You may agree and think yes, we should
study our Mr Pritchard and learn our rhyme and metre and go quietly
about the business of achieving other ambitions. Well, I have a secret for
you. Huddle up ... Huddle UP! We don't read and write poetry because it's
cute. We read and write poetry because we are members of the human
race. And the human race is filled with passion. Medicine, law, business:
these are all noble pursuits necessary to sustain life. But poetry, beauty,
romance, and love—these are what we stay alive for. To quote from
Whitman: 'O me! O life! Of the question of these recurring. Of the endless
trains of the faithless, of cities fill'd with the foolish. What good amid these?
O me, O life? Answer. That you are here, that life exists, and identity. The
powerful play goes on, and you may contribute a verse.' The powerful play
goes on and you may contribute a verse. What will your verse be?

-- Robin Williams, Dead Poets Society

485.

Will you listen very, very carefully to me? Just for once? This may be
the last time I ever talk to you. Not everyone in this world is after your
magnificent body, lady. In the first place, it's not so magnificent. It's fair,
but it ain't keeping me up nights, you know? I don't even think you're very
pretty. Maybe if you smiled once in awhile, okay, but I don't want you to do
anything against your religion. And you are not the only person in this city
ever to get dumped on. I myself am a recent dumpee. I am a dedicated
actor, Paula, you know? I am dedicated to my art and my craft. I value what

113

I do. And because of a mentally arthritic director, I am about to play the second greatest role in the history of the English-speaking theatre like a double order of fresh California fruit salad. When I say 'nice' I mean 'nice', ya know: decent, fair. I deserve it, because I'm a nice, decent, and fair person. I don't wanna jump on your bones. I don't even want to see you in the morning. But I'll tell you what I do like about you, Paula: Lucy. Lucy's your best part. Lucy is worth putting up with you for. So here is fourteen dollars for the care and feeding of that terrific kid. You get ziiiip-ity-doo-dah! You want any money? Borrow it from your ten-year-old daughter. I am now going inside my room to meditate away my hostility toward you. Personally, I don't think it can be done.

-- Richard Dreyfuss, *The Goodbye Girl*
(standing up to his infuriating flatmate. Dreyfuss won an Oscar for this.)

486.
You love playing with that. You love playing with all your stuffed animals. You love your Mommy, your Daddy. You love your pyjamas. You love everything, don't you? Yeah. But you know what, buddy? As you get older, some of the things you love might not seem so special anymore. Like your Jack-in-the-Box. Maybe you'll realise it's just a piece of tin and a stuffed animal. And then you forget the few things you really love. And by the time you get to my age, maybe it's only one or two things. With me, I think it's one.

-- Jeremy Renner, *The Hurt Locker*
(to his son)

487.
My father was a relentlessly self-improving boulangerie owner from Belgium with low-grade narcolepsy and a penchant for buggery. My mother was a 15-year-old French prostitute named Chloe with webbed feet. My father would womanise, he would drink, he would make outrageous claims like he invented the question mark. Sometimes, he would accuse chestnuts of being lazy—the sort of general malaise that

only the genius possess and the insane lament. My childhood was typical: summers in Rangoon, luge lessons. In the spring, we'd make meat helmets. When I was insolent, I was placed in a burlap bag and beaten with reeds. Pretty standard, really. At the age of twelve, I received my first scribe. At the age of fourteen, a Zoroastrian woman named Vilma ritualistically shaved my testicles. There really is nothing like a shorn scrotum, it's breathtaking. I suggest you try it.

-- Mike Myers, *Austin Powers: International Man of Mystery*
(as Dr Evil)

488.

Uh, well, I tell ya, I remember this one time. I'm in a Banshee at night in combat conditions, so there's no running lights on the carrier. It was the Shangri-La, and we were in the Sea of Japan, and my, my radar had jammed, and my homing signal was gone ... because somebody in Japan was actually using the same frequency. And so it was, it was leading me away from where I was supposed to be. And I'm lookin' down at a big, black ocean, so I flip on my map light and then, suddenly, zap! Everything shorts out right there in my cockpit. All my instruments are gone. My lights are gone. And I can't even tell now what my altitude is. I know I'm running out of fuel, so I'm thinking about ditching in the ocean. And I, I look down there, and then, in, in the darkness, there's this green trail. It's like a long carpet that's just laid out right beneath me. And it was the algae, right? It was that phosphorescent stuff that gets churned up in the wake of a big ship. And it was, it was, it was just leading me home. You know? If my cockpit lights hadn't shorted out, there's no way I'd have ever been able to see that. So, uh, you, uh, you never know what... what events are going to transpire to get you home.

-- Tom Hanks, *Apollo 13*

489.

The key to faking out the parents is the clammy hands. It's a good non-specific symptom. A lot of people will tell you that a phoney fever is a dead lock, but if you get a nervous mother, you could land in the doctor's office. That's worse than school. What you do is you fake a stomach cramp, and when you're bent over, moaning and wailing, you lick your palms. It's a little childish and stupid, but then, so is high school. I did have a test today. That wasn't bullshit. It's on European socialism. I mean, really, what's the point? I'm not European, I don't plan on being European, so who gives a crap if they're socialist? They could be fascist anarchists—that still wouldn't change the fact that I don't own a car. Not that I condone fascism, or any ism for that matter. Isms, in my opinion, are not good. A person should not believe in an ism—he should believe in himself. I quote John Lennon: 'I don't believe in The Beatles. I just believe in me.' A good point there. Of course, he was the Walrus. I could be the Walrus—I'd still have to bum rides off of people.

-- Matthew Broderick, *Ferris Bueller's Day Off*
(The opening narration)

490.

I've been thinking about something Dumbledore said to me. That even though we've got a fight ahead of us, we've got one thing that Voldemort doesn't have: something worth fighting for.

-- Daniel Radcliffe, *Harry Potter and the Order of the Phoenix*
(last lines)

491.

But, those ... those things she told you I did to her? Who ... who ... who else was going to love me? WHO else was going to touch me? WHO else was going to make me feel good about myself?

-- Mo'Nique, *Precious*
(about why she allowed her partner to abuse her daughter)

492.

Is Rome worth one good man's life? We believed it once. Make us believe it again ... He was a soldier of Rome. Honour him!

-- Connie Nielsen, *Gladiator*

493.

Oh Jerry, don't let's ask for the moon. We have the stars.

-- Bette Davis, *Now, Voyager*

494.

I got an idea for a movie.

-- John Travolta, *Get Shorty*

495.

The National Science Foundation invited me even though I made it clear I would not be making another movie about penguins.

-- Werner Herzog, *Encounters at the End of the World*

496.

There were too many of us, we had access to too much equipment, too much money, and little by little we went insane.

-- Francis Ford Coppola, *Hearts of Darkness*

497.

My films happen because I sign a contract. I get an advance that I don't want to repay, so I have to make the film.

-- Federico Fellini, *Fellini: I am a Born Liar*

498.
What we professional liars hope to serve is truth. I'm afraid the pompous word for that is 'art'.

-- Orson Welles, *F for Fake*

499.
People used to stare at fires. Now they watch TV. We need to see moving images, especially after dinner.

-- Francois Truffaut, *Day for Night*

500.
I'm giving her all she's got, Captain!

-- Simon Pegg, *Star Trek* (2009)

Un-quotes

The following are said to be famous quotes, but they are not. Mostly, they're just a little off, but in some cases their origins are completely mysterious. Nevertheless, each is as famous as the celebrity it attempts to honour:

★ 'Play it again, Sam'. This is attributed to Bogart in *Casablanca*. What was actually said was 'Play it! If she can stand it, I can.' Similarly, Ingrid Bergman said, 'Play it, Sam. Play "As Time Goes By"'.

★ 'You dirty rat', by James Cagney. He said different combinations at times—'that dirty double-crossin' rat' (in *Blonde Crazy*), 'You dirty yellow-bellied rat' (*Taxi!*). So, he didn't say it, *per se*. But the Three Stooges did say it. Often.

★ 'Come viz me to ze Kasbah,' so pleaded Charles Boyer, apparently, in *Algiers*. But he never did say it, in any form, in any film.

★ 'I vant to be alone,' by Greta Garbo. She's said, 'We want to be alone' (in *Ninotchka*) and 'I vant to be left alone' (in *Grand Hotel*).

★ 'Judy, Judy, Judy.' Cary Grant never said it.

★ 'Everybody wants to get into the act,' is a famous line used by mimics to impersonate Jimmy Durante. An example is Mel Blanc in the Tweety Bird vehicle *A Gruesome Twosome*. Durante only ever said it on television—specifically *The Jimmy Durante Show*—so unfortunately it doesn't qualify as a quote from film, unless you want to credit Mel Blanc.

★ 'You feelin' lucky, punk?' by Clint Eastwood, *Dirty Harry*. The correct quote is 'You gotta ask yourself one question. Do I feel lucky? Well Do ya? Punk.'

★ 'Me Tarzan. You Jane.' Tarzan not say this. Say something else.

★ 'Greed is good' from *Wall Street*. The Greed is Good motto is similar to the maxims, 'possession is nine points of the law' or, 'the love of money is the root of all evil,' in that through frequent misquoting or missed context it's attained a meaning opposite to its origins. Compare the suggestion of 'greed is good' (being a despicable, money-hungry mantra) with what he's actually saying, 'Greed, for lack of a better word, is good. Greed, in all its forms, greed for life, money, love, knowledge—has marked the upward surge of mankind.'

★ 'This is another fine mess you've gotten me into.' So go the famous words supposedly spoken by Oliver Hardy to Stan Laurel. The correct quote is 'Well here's another nice mess you've gotten me into', but the film's title, *Another Fine Mess*, might have something to do with the confusion.

★ 'Come up and see me some time,' by Mae West. The film was *She Done Him Wrong*, and the correct quote is 'Why don't you come up some time and see me?'.

★ 'I want to suck your blood,' Dracula would say to you, as apparently made famous by Bela Lugosi. However, he never did say it.

★ 'Beam me up, Scotty.' Supposedly said by William Shatner throughout *Star Trek*, in fact, this was never said at all. Although he did get close in the fourth film with 'Scotty, beam me up'. As it turns out, the line was already as famous as the television series in which it never appeared.

Quizzes

Welcome to the quiz pages! For each correct answer to a question, you receive one point. While some of the questions will seem really tough, they're supposed to be. Others are also really easy.

The answers appear on pages 133–137. Keep a tally as you go and when you get to the final page, add them and find out whether you're movie mad or just celluloid silly.

Have fun and good luck!

Quiz # 1
Say that Again

These are recurring quotes from certain actors. They are phrases that keep popping up, in their lines, in their films, out of their mouths. Sometimes the line's always in, and sometimes they can't help themselves. Who are they?

1. Oh ... my ... God!
2. I'll be back.
3. Oh, you're unbelievable!
4. Must go faster!
5. I'm just gettin' warmed up.
6. Yippee-ki-ya, motherfucker.
7. Vodka martini. Shaken, not stirred.
8. But of course you are.
9. This is some repugnant shit!
10. I'm too old for this shit.

Quiz # 2
Pardon my French

The following five quotes are taken from the English subtitles of some of the great foreign films. In fact, they're from the quills of five of the master directors of world cinema. Following the quote is the actor's name, the country of origin and the decade of release. Your job is to earn two points: one for the name of the film and one for the director. By the way, even for a serious student of film, these are tough. Just getting one point would be good work.

1. I met Death today. We are playing chess.
    -- Max von Sydow, Sweden in the middle ages; the 1950s

2. A serpent's egg is white and pure. A bird's is speckled and soiled. The bird left the speckled egg for the white. The egg cracks; out comes a snake. The bird is gobbled by the snake. Stupid bird.
    -- Peter, feudal Japan; the 1980s

3. We have no ambition to conquer any cosmos. We just want to extend Earth up to the Cosmos' borders. We don't want any more worlds, only a mirror to see our own. We try so hard to make contact, but we're doomed to failure. We look ridiculous pursuing a goal we fear and that we really don't need. Man needs man!
    -- Juri Jarvet, the USSR in future space-exploration; the 1970s

4. There's no need to lie. It's like poker. The truth is best. The others still think you're bluffing, so you win.
    -- Jean Paul Belmondo, France in the fifties; the 1960s

5. You see, what stands out at a first reading is the lack of a central issue or a philosophical stance. That makes the film a chain of gratuitous episodes which may even be amusing in their ambivalent realism. You wonder, what is the director really trying to do? Make us think? Scare us? That ploy betrays a basic lack of poetic inspiration.

    -- Jean Rouguel, Italy in the sixties; the 1960s

Quiz # 3
Join the Dots

Count the dots in the sentence to help find the film title. For example, from quite a few pages back, Gregory Peck completed the following sentence: "I could shoot all the blue jays I wanted, if I could hit 'em, but it was a sin ../...../../........." (2, 4, 1, 11).

The answer is 'to kill a mockingbird'. Each dot represents a letter in the word, and the bracketed numerals show the number of letters in each word.

Some tips:
a) Use American spellings, as in the official title of the film
b) Generally, a one- or three-letter word is either an article ('a', 'the') or a pronoun ('I', 'you'). There is only one exception: in one of the questions none of the three-letter words are pronouns or articles.
c) Numbers are spelt.

1. 1. I think it pisses God off when you walk by .../...../...... in a field and don't notice it. (3, 5, 6)

    -- Margaret Avery to Whoopi Goldberg.

2. I have given a name to my pain, and it is ...... (6)

    -- Jack Nicholson, in heavy make-up, sotto voce.

3. Oh yeah? Well at least I'm not ..../.../..... out from under her! (9, 3, 5)

    -- Danny DeVito to Michael Douglas.

4. You were in the window. You waved to me. 'Bye bye, .../..., bye bye'. (4, 3)

    -- Dustin Hoffman.

5. Dr Grant, my dear Dr Sattler. Welcome to ..../.... (8, 4)

    -- Richard Attenborough.

6. The ..../....../....... was dedicated to sucking the marrow out of life. (4, 5, 7)

    -- Robin Williams to Ethan Hawke and others.

7. What is the victory of a .../../.../.../....? (3, 2, 1, 3, 3, 4)

    -- Paul Newman. Elizabeth Taylor answers, 'Just stayin' on, I guess.'

8. I took the Kaiser blade, some folks call it a ...../....., I call it a Kaiser Blade. (5, 5)

    -- Billy Bob Thornton.

9. They usually call death row the last mile, but we called ours .../...../.... because the floor was the colour of faded limes. (3, 5, 4)

    -- Dabbs Greer.

10. So you see, she knew I was gonna lead the army of the ....../....... into the pages of history before it ever even occurred to me. (6, 7)

    -- Brad Pitt to Bruce Willis.

11. Next Saturday night, we're sending you ..../../.../...... (4, 2, 3, 6)

    -- Christopher Lloyd to Michael J Fox.

12. Peter once asked me when it was that I fell in love with Jack, and I told him it was ...../.../..../....... (5, 3, 4, 8)

    -- Sandra Bullock, narrating.

13. Oh, Luke. He was some boy, .../..../.... —hell, he's a natural-born world-shaker. (4, 4, 4)

    -- George Kennedy.

Quiz # 4
Coup de Grace

Name the films where the deathblow (by bullet, bomb, suicide, etc.) was struck on the delivery of these lines. Note: the blow was not necessarily struck by the assailant.

1. You're all clear, kid. Now let's blow this thing and go home. (Ship's cannon)

2. Smile, you son of a— *(Rifle shot)*

3. Goodbye, Leo Crow. *(Pistol shot)*

4. ... Smith, Wesson and me. *(Several pistol shots)*

5. This is from... Matilda. *(Grenade explosion)*

6. Have you ever danced with the devil by the pale moonlight? *(Pistol shot)*

7. We are the Judean People's Front crack suicide squad! Suicide squad, attack! *(Knife)*

8. Take *this* under advisement, jerkweed. *(Bomb)*

9. Become vengeance, David. Become wrath. *(Pistol shot)*

10. Take me! Come into me! God damn you! Take me! Take me! *(Suicide leap)*

Quiz # 5
Once More, with Feeling

Throughout which films are the following lines repeated?

1. Spared no expense.
   -- Richard Attenborough

2. Be excellent to each other ... and party on, dudes!
   -- Keanu Reeves and Alex Winter

3. Etcetera, etcetera, etcetera.
   -- Yul Brynner

4. Awful tired now, boss. Dog tired.
   -- Michael Clarke Duncan

5. Hoo-ah!
   -- Al Pacino

6. You're terrible, Muriel!
   -- Gabby Milgate

7. Willkommen. Bienvenue. Welcome. C'mon in.
   -- Madeline Kahn

8. We were like peas and carrots, Jenny and I.
   -- Tom Hanks

9. Push the button, Max!
   -- Jack Lemmon

10. There can be only one!
    -- Sean Connery and Christopher Lambert

11. Inconceivable!
    -- Wallace Shawn

12. You've got red on you.
    -- Simon Pegg and others

Quiz # 6
Tag Lines

Name the films for which the following were media or poster blurbs. To assist you, they are in chronological order from the late 1960s.

1. Not that it matters, but most of it is true.
2. You don't assign him to murder cases. You just turn him loose.
3. Hell, upside down.
4. One tiny spark becomes a night of blazing suspense.
5. His whole life was a million-to-one shot.
6. A long time ago, in a galaxy far, far away...
7. Just when you thought it was safe to go back in the water.
8. You'll believe a man can fly.
9. In space, no-one can hear you scream.
10. The human adventure is just beginning.
11. Man is the warmest place to hide.
12. Be afraid. Be very afraid.
13. The first casualty of war is innocence.
14. An adventure 65 million years in the making.
15. Fear can hold you prisoner. Hope can set you free.
16. Five criminals. One line-up. No coincidence.
17. Collide with destiny.
18. The mission is a man.
19. Look closer.
20. A hero will rise.
21. Let the magic begin.
22. The eighth wonder of the world!
23. No children. No future. No hope.
24. An adventure beyond the ordinar-E.

Quiz # 7:
Last Lines

The following are the last lines of films and the actor who spoke them. Your task is to name the film. These appear difficult but most have in common a form of notoriety for the actor.

1.   ... and a vial of insulin please ... Just kidding.

-- Jeremy Irons

2.   Well, nobody's perfect.

-- Joe E Brown

3.   You have no idea what I'm talking about, I'm sure. But, don't worry, you will someday.

-- Kevin Spacey

4.   So long, architect.

-- Steve McQueen

5.   If this is their idea of Christmas, I GOT to be here for New Year.

-- DeVereaux White.

6.   And now we are free. I will see you again, but not yet. Not yet.

-- Djimon Hounsou

7.   I think I'll have a drink.

-- Kevin Costner.

8.   My God. What have I done?

-- Alec Guinness.

9.   Welcome to the New World, sir.

-- Alec Baldwin

10. Well, I guess that's pretty much how I feel about relationships, y'know, they're totally irrational and crazy and absurd and, but, uh, I guess we keep going through it because, uh, most of us need the eggs.

-- Woody Allen

11. They're coming for you! YOU'RE NEXT!

-- Kevin McCarthy

12. Nah. I'd only blow it.

-- *Robert Redford*

13. Watch the skies, everywhere! Keep looking. Keep watching the skies!

-- *Douglas Spencer*

14. Forget it, Jake. It's Chinatown.

-- *Joe Mantell*

15. There's nothing to forgive, Sydney.

-- *Hang S. Ngor*

16. For a minute there I thought we were in trouble.

-- *Robert Redford*

17. I can't imagine why.

-- *Richard Dreyfuss*

18. Why don't we just wait here for a while... see what happens.

-- Kurt Russell

19. Now, where was I?

-- Guy Pearce

20. I say these words as a prayer, as regret, as praise, I say: Lowenstein, Lowenstein.

-- Nick Nolte

21. **You're making me angry. You wouldn't like me when I'm angry.**

-- Eric Bana

22. **Well Tillie, when the hell are we going to get some dinner?**

-- Spencer Tracy

23. **Shut up and deal.**

-- Shirley MacLaine

# Quiz Answers

Keep a tally of your score and proceed to the final page to see how you fared.

Quiz #1, **Say that Again**. One point for each actor named correctly:
1. Charlton Heston (in nearly everything).
2. Arnold Schwarzenegger, first in *The Terminator*, then seven others, plus one variation: 'She'll be back,' from Terminator 3: Rise of the Machines.
3. Kurt Russell
4. Jeff Goldblum in *Jurassic Park* and *Independence Day*.
5. Al Pacino in *Scent of a Woman* and *The Devil's Advocate*
6. Bruce Willis in all *Die Hard* films
7. Sean Connery (and others) in nearly all *Bond* films
8. Sean Connery in *Diamonds Are Forever*, *Rising Sun*, *The Rock*.
9. Samuel L Jackson in *Jackie Brown*, *Pulp Fiction*, *Shaft*
10. Danny Glover in *Lethal Weapon* 1 to 4 and *Maverick*

Quiz #2, **Pardon my French**. There are two points on offer. Earn one for the film, and one for the director:
1. *The Seventh Seal,* Ingmar Bergman
2. *Ran*, Akira Kurosawa
3. *Solyaris (Solaris)*, Andre Tarkovsky
4. A bout de souffle (Breathless), Jean-Luc Godard
5. 8½ , Federico Fellini

Quiz #3, **Join the Dots**. One point each:
1. *The Color Purple*
2. *Batman*
3. *Romancing the Stone*
4. *Rain Man*
5. *Jurassic Park*
6. *Dead Poets Society*
7. *Cat on a Hot Tin Roof*
8. *Sling Blade*
9. *The Green Mile*
10. *Twelve Monkeys*
11. *Back to the Future*
12. *While You were Sleeping*
13. *Cool Hand Luke*

Quiz #4, **Coup de Grace**. One point each for the film only.
1. *Star Wars*, Harrison Ford at the end
2. *Jaws*, Roy Scheider, at the end of the film, shooting the scuba tank
3. *Minority Report,* the repeated pre-cog. sequence of Tom Cruise finding his son's kidnapper
4. *Sudden Impact*, Clint Eastwood in the coffee shop in response to the burglar demanding, 'Who's we, sucker?'
5. *Leon* (aka The Professional), Jean Reno
6. *Batman*, Jack Nicholson
7. *Life of Brian*, by an unidentified cast-member to Brian, who's on the cross
8. *Die Hard*, Bruce Willis, as he places a bomb on an office chair and pushes it towards the open elevator shaft
9. *Se7en*, Kevin Spacey at the end
10. *The Exorcist*, Jason Miller at the end

Quiz #5, **Once More, with Feeling**. One point for each correct answer:

1. *Jurassic Park*
2. *Bill and Ted's Excellent Adventure*
3. *The King and I*
4. *The Green Mile*
5. *Scent of a Woman*
6. *Muriel's Wedding*
7. *Blazing Saddles*
8. *Forrest Gump*
9. *The Great Race*
10. *Highlander*
11. *The Princess Bride*
12. *Shaun of the Dead*

Quiz #6, **Tag Lines**. One point:

1. *Butch Cassidy and The Sundance Kid*
2. *Dirty Harry*
3. *The Poseidon Adventure*
4. *The Towering Inferno*
5. *Rocky*
6. *Star Wars*
7. *Jaws 2*
8. *Superman: The Movie*
9. *Alien*
10. *Star Trek: The Motion Picture*
11. *The Thing*
12. *The Fly (1986)*
13. *Platoon*
14. *Jurassic Park*
15. *The Shawshank Redemption*

16. *The Usual Suspects*
17. *Titanic*
18. *Saving Private Ryan*
19. *American Beauty*
20. *Gladiator*
21. *Harry Potter and the Philosopher's Stone*
22. *King Kong*
23. *Children of Men*
24. *Wall-E*

Quiz #7, **Last Lines.** One point each

1. *Reversal of Fortune*
2. *Some Like it Hot*
3. *American Beauty*
4. *The Towering Inferno*
5. *Die Hard*
6. *Gladiator*
7. *The Untouchables*
8. *The Bridge on the River Kwai*
9. *The Hunt for Red October*
10. *Annie Hall*
11. *Invasion of the Body Snatchers*
12. *The Sting*
13. *The Thing from Another World*
14. *Chinatown*
15. *The Killing Fields*
16. *Butch Cassidy and the Sundance Kid*
17. *Jaws*
18. *The Thing*
19. *Memento*
20. *Prince of Tides*

21. *Hulk*
22. *Guess Who's Coming to Dinner*
23. *The Apartment*

Your Quiz Tally

There were 100 points available. So, how did you score?

0 to 15
TV Watcher

You are the film-viewer version of Ed Wood (*Plan 9 from Outer Space*): the mere fact that you're involved shows promise. Well played.

16 to 30
Movie goer

If you were a film director, you'd be Brett Ratner (*Rush Hour*): you know a bit, but could do much better—there's a lot more to film than just modern Hollywood.

31 to 55
Cinema lover

Frank Darabont (*The Shawshank Redemption, The Green Mile*) is you when he's not making films: skilled and respected, but not involved enough or capable of the right choices to be amongst the elite.

56 to 70
Film fan

Well done, Quentin Tarantino. You have shown panache and technical proficiency, and pulled off some bravura moments, but perhaps just lacking an artistic sense.

71 to 90
Cineaste

John Huston and Ridley Scott would be proud of you. Like them, you are the Go To person for all things film. The only thing stopping you from being in the top rank is time.

91 to 100
Academy president

You must have seen and remembered every movie there is. You can discuss film history, art-house cinema and pop-corn flicks with equal passion. Genius. You are Orson Welles. Or Alfred Hitchcock depending on your preference. At your level you can be whomever you wish.

Index

THE

END

My favourite film quotes

_____

_____

_____

_____

_____

_____

_____

_____

_____

_____

_____

My favourite film quotes

_____

_____

_____

_____

_____

_____

_____

_____

_____

_____

_____

_____

_____

First published in Australia in 2010 by
New Holland Publishers (Australia) Pty Ltd
Sydney • Auckland • London • Cape Town

1/66 Gibbes Street Chatswood NSW 2067 Australia
218 Lake Road Northcote Auckland New Zealand
86 Edgware Road London W2 2EA United Kingdom
80 McKenzie Street Cape Town 8001 South Africa

The 500 greatest film quotes ever / Steve Odgers.
9781742570150 (pbk.)
Includes index.
Motion pictures--Quotations, maxims, etc
791.43

Publisher: Linda Williams
Publishing Manager: Lliane Clarke
Editor: Rochelle Fernandez
Designer: Amanda Tarlau
Production Manager: Olga Dementiev
Printed and bound in India by Replika Press Pvt. Ltd.
10 9 8 7 6 5 4 3 2 1